BLUEPRINTS
The Spelling Book

Laura Huxford

D. Whyte.

Stanley Thornes (Publishers) Ltd

Do you receive *BLUEPRINTS NEWS*?

Blueprints is an expanding series of practical teacher's ideas books and photocopiable resources for use in primary schools. Books are available for separate infant and junior age ranges for every core and foundation subject, as well as for an ever widening range of other primary teaching needs. These include **Blueprints Primary English** books and **Blueprints Resource Banks**. **Blueprints** are carefully structured around the demands of the National Curriculum in England and Wales, but are used successfully by schools and teachers in Scotland, Northern Ireland and elsewhere.

Blueprints provide:

●   *Total curriculum coverage*
●   *Hundreds of practical ideas*
●   *Books specifically for the age range you teach*
●   *Flexible resources for the whole school or for individual teachers*
●   *Excellent photocopiable sheets – ideal for assessment and children's work profiles*
●   *Supreme value.*

Books may be bought by credit card over the telephone and information obtained on (**01242**) **577944**. Alternatively, photocopy and return this **FREEPOST** form to receive **Blueprints News**, our regular update on all new and existing titles. You may also like to add the name of a friend who would be interested in being on the mailing list.

Please add my name to the **BLUEPRINTS NEWS** mailing list.

Mr/Mrs/Miss/Ms _____

Home address _____

_____ Postcode _____

School address _____

_____ Postcode _____

Please also send **BLUEPRINTS NEWS** to:

Mr/Mrs/Miss/Ms _____

Address _____

_____ Postcode _____

To: Marketing Services Dept., Stanley Thornes Ltd, FREEPOST (GR 782), Cheltenham, GL50 1BR

First published in 1994 by:
Stanley Thornes (Publishers) Ltd
Ellenborough House
Wellington Street
CHELTENHAM GL50 1YW
England

A catalogue record for this book is available from the British Library.

ISBN 0–7487–1812–5

Typeset by Tech-Set, Gateshead, Tyne & Wear.
Printed in Great Britain.

96 97 98 99 00 / 10 9 8 7 6 5 4 3

CONTENTS

Preface   **iv**
  What is Blueprints *The Spelling Book?*   iv
  About this book   v
  How to use this book   v
  Use of copymasters   vi
  List of copymasters   vii

Introduction: Spelling should be taught   **viii**
  The principles on which the teaching suggestions are made   viii
  Learning to write   ix
  Learning to spell   x
  Teaching spelling   xi

Part 1   Beginning to spell   **1**

Assessment   2
  Sounds   2
  Letters   3

Teaching beginning spelling   4
  Hearing initial sounds in words   4
  Letters   5
  Rhyming   8
  Hearing final sounds in words   9
  Hearing short vowels in words   10
  Long vowels   12
  Hearing consonant blends in words   12
  The alphabet   13

Copymasters 1–93

Part 2   Later spelling   **107**

Assessment   108
  Assessments 1–3   108
  Assessments 4–6   112

Teaching later spelling   115
  Letter-strings   115
  More letter-strings   118
  Further spelling practice   119

Copymasters 94–118

Further reading   146

PREFACE

What is Blueprints *The Spelling Book*?

The Spelling Book is a complete developmental programme for teaching spelling in primary schools. It is based on a coherent analysis of recent research into spelling and enables you to offer children a carefully thought out progression of spelling activities.

The book is divided into two parts:

- Part 1 Beginning to spell
- Part 2 Later spelling.

It provides 118 photocopiable sheets and a wide range of activities, including:

- diagnostic assessments
- worksheets
- a wide variety of games to play, including lotto, track games, dominoes and other matching games.

Many of the copymasters contain banks of pictures, letters or words which can be made up and mounted for permanent use. (You will find suggestions for doing this on page vi.)

The key to using the book is in the diagnostic assessments at the beginning of Parts 1 and 2. You will find it helpful to read introductory pages v and vi, before proceeding further. They provide you with a simple strategy for placing children on the programme. You will also find it valuable to read pages viii–xi which explain simply the development of spelling skills and which provide the structure of the book. Once you start on one of the two sections, you will need to read the teacher's notes at the front.

The Spelling Book covers all the needs of primary school children for the National Curriculum and the corresponding levels of English 5–14 for Scotland. Using this programme, children can attain National Curriculum Level 5/6 and Level D in Scotland.

ABOUT THIS BOOK

The book is divided into two parts.

Part 1 Beginning to spell contains procedures for assessing and teaching:

a) ability to hear initial, final, medial and consonant blend sounds in words

b) knowledge of letter–sound correspondence.

Part 2 Later spelling contains:

a) procedures for assessing and teaching the following most frequently used words in the language:

about	day	is	our	they
after	do	last	out	this
all	down	like	over	three
and	for	little	play	too
are	from	made	put	two
away	go	make	said	us
back	has	me	saw	very
be	have	my	she	want
because	he	next	so	was
by	her	new	some	we
call	here	off	take	were
came	his	old	their	when
come	home	once	then	will
could	I	one	there	you

b) specific suggestions for teaching another sixty of the most frequently used words

c) general suggestions for teaching spelling.

HOW TO USE THIS BOOK

Take a piece of writing which the child has completed without assistance from either an adult or a word bank. Compare it with the examples given below.

In the first two examples there is no relationship between the marks on the page and the words. The child in example 3 was unable to hear vowels in words and so represented only the first and last sounds. Children whose writing has similar features to those in examples 1–3 should be assessed using the procedures in Part 1 Beginning to spell.

1.	2.	3.
		I LᶜDSwt Rachel wyHv TTsGTᴀⅅTSⅴ PSᴀDTGLɔ
…and the little pig said 'by the hair on my chinny chin chin, I will not let you in.'	*The workmen are building the house. They make cement in the cement mixer.*	*I like dancing with Rachel. We have tutus – gold and silver; points and gallops.*

4.	5.
The wih mil glds the con into Padre suf wis is cod flow and wey yos it to mac cocs aha teh wen the con is grid it is sod insid	Wednesday 21th september the little owl his Beak anl witt feathers its hed tuks rit rad and his clor are vere srpp and his eye are gren .
The windmill grinds the corn into powder stuff which is called flour, and we use it to make cakes and then when the corn is ground it is stored inside.	*the little owl his beak and with feathers its head turns right round and his claws are very sharp and his eye are green* (spellings of 'beak', 'feathers' and 'eye' were on display)

Examples 4 and 5 indicate that the children can hear three or more sounds in words. There are also instances of correctly spelled common words, e.g. 'and', 'the' and 'are'. Children whose writing has similar features to those in these examples or whose spelling is more advanced should be assessed using the procedures in Part 2   Later spelling.

The assessment procedures in Part 1 and Part 2 are each followed by instructions for a teaching programme.

Children require no reading ability in order to pursue the teaching programmes in Part I   Beginning spelling, and only a limited reading ability is required for the teaching programmes in Part II   Later spelling.

USE OF COPYMASTERS

The copymasters in this book consist of worksheets or materials for activities or games. Many contain banks of pictures, letters or words. For most activities, the instructions state that these should be cut out and stuck on to small cards. Blank playing cards are ideal for this purpose and can be obtained from Taskmaster Ltd, Morris Road, Clarendon Park, Leicester LE2 6BR. It would save time if the copymasters could be photo-copied on to self-adhesive address labels. It is also quicker to photocopy baseboards directly on to A4 card if the photocopier will take thick enough card. Where copymasters have to be cut up, the individual items are numbered separately so that if cards become mixed up, they can easily be re-sorted. If a game is made up for permanent use, it is worth colouring in the pictures with brightly coloured felt pens. The children will enjoy doing this in wet playtimes. The baseboards can also be covered with sticky-back plastic.

LIST OF COPYMASTERS

1   Pictures for assessing final vowel and middle sounds
2   Pictures for assessing initial consonant blends
3   Test card for assessing letter knowledge (1)
4   Test card for assessing letter knowledge (2)
5   Hearing initial sounds 's' (1)
6   Hearing initial sounds 's' (2)
7   Hearing initial sounds – odd-one-out
8   Hearing initial sounds – matching
9   Matching letters – c o a d g e f s
10 Matching letters – g and a
11 Matching letters – d, f and c
12 Matching activity – letter bank (1)
13 Matching activity – letter bank (2)
14 Matching activity – baseboard
15 Matching activity – picture bank (1)
16 Matching activity – picture bank (2)
17 Dominoes – c o a d g e f s qu
18 Picture bank – b p r n m h k l t j i u w y v z sh ch th (1)
19 Picture bank – b p r n m h k l t j i u w y v z sh ch th (2)
20 Picture bank – b p r n m h k l t j i u w y v z sh ch th (3)
21 Picture bank – b p r n m h k l t j i u w y v z sh ch th (4)
22 Practice – sh ch
23 Track game – h t l b w r v n k (1)
24 Track game – h t l b w r v n k (2)
25 Lotto – b p r n m h l t j i u w v sh ch th (1)
26 Lotto – b p r n m h l t j i u w v sh ch th (2)
27 Dominoes – b p r n m h k l t i u v
28 Writing initial letters – a e i o u
29 Choosing initial letters (1)
30 Choosing initial letters (2)
31 Animal letters game (baseboard 1) – f w s a l b
32 Animal letters game (baseboard 2) – z k e m h o
33 Animal letters game (baseboard 3) – p c d r t g
34 Post boxes (1) – c a d
35 Post boxes (2) – l h b
36 Rhyming picture bank (1)
37 Rhyming picture bank (2)
38 Rhyming worksheet (1)
39 Rhyming worksheet (2)
40 Blank templates for track game (1)
41 Blank templates for track game (2)
42 Picture bank – final sounds – k d j ing l
43 Picture bank – final sounds – l s n t
44 Sorting pictures – final sounds baseboard
45 Odd-one-out – final sound
46 Final 'l' sound
47 Beginning and end sound dominoes
48 Matching pictures to letters – n t
49 Practice writing – b p d
50 Matching pictures to letters: final sounds – g d p
51 Matching pictures to words: distinguishing final sounds
52 Making beginnings and ends of words (1)
53 Making beginnings and ends of words (2)
54 Picture bank – middle vowel (1)
55 Picture bank – middle vowel (2)
56 Picture bank – middle vowel (3)
57 Matching pictures – middle vowel (1)
58 Matching pictures – middle vowel (2)
59 Matching words to pictures – middle vowel

60 Writing middle vowels a e
61 Writing middle vowels o u
62 Matching pictures to letters – middle vowels a i e
63 Matching pictures to letters – middle vowels a e i o u
64 Writing middle vowels – i e
65 Writing middle vowels – a e i o u
66 Writing three-letter words
67 Writing three- and four- letter words
68 Crossword
69 Matching and writing words (1)
70 Matching and writing words (2)
71 Writing ends of words (1)
72 Writing ends of words (2)
73 Long vowel lotto (1) – cards
74 Long vowel lotto (1) – baseboard
75 Long vowel lotto (2) – cards
76 Long vowel lotto (2) – baseboard
77 Long vowel lotto (3) – cards
78 Long vowel lotto (3) – baseboard
79 Matching pictures to consonant blends – pictures
80 Matching pictures to consonant blends – baseboard (1)
81 Matching pictures to consonant blends – baseboard (2)
82 Matching pictures to 's' blends – pictures
83 Matching pictures to 's' blends – baseboard
84 Maze game 's' blends
85 Picture activity 's' blends
86 Writing second consonants
87 Matching words to pictures – distinguishing final consonant blends
88 Writing words – initial and final consonant blends
89 Dot-to-dot – lower-case letters (1)
90 Dot-to-dot – lower-case letters (2)
91 Dot-to-dot – upper-case letters (1)
92 Dot-to-dot – upper-case letters (2)
93 Matching upper- to lower- case letters
94 Later spelling assessment – Martha's house
95 Later spelling assessment – On the bus to the zoo
96 Later spelling assessment – The man with the balloons
97 Later spelling assessment – Sale poster
98 Later spelling assessment – The rabbits I
99 Later spelling assessment – The rabbits II
100 Blank template for worksheet
101 Picture bank for use with Copymaster 100
102 Letter-string 'the'
103 Words within words
104 Letter-string 'one'
105 Letter-string 'own'
106 Letter-string 'one' and 'own'
107 Spelling game I (1)
108 Spelling game I (2)
109 Spelling game I (3)
110 Spelling game II (1)
111 Spelling game II (2)
112 Strings game (1)
113 Strings game (2)
114 Strings game (3)
115 Strings game (4)
116 Strings game (5)
117 Prefix and suffix wheels (1)
118 Prefix and suffix wheels (2)

INTRODUCTION: SPELLING SHOULD BE TAUGHT

Much recent research into spelling has led to the conclusion that spelling should be taught and that merely testing children's ability to spell a list of words they have taken home to memorise does not constitute 'teaching spelling'.

When deciding how to teach spelling, we need to consider its function, attitudes to it, the structure of words, and children's development and learning styles. Research into these aspects of spelling is as yet limited. Children's early spelling has probably received the most attention. The suggestions made in this book are based on this research and current practice in schools. You will find a list of books in which the research can be found on page 146.

THE PRINCIPLES ON WHICH THE TEACHING SUGGESTIONS ARE MADE

Spelling is not an end in itself. It is one of a number of skills required in the process of writing
The purpose of writing is not to spell. It is to communicate or record ideas or information. More important than spelling is choosing and organising words to express exactly what we wish to say, e.g. to give precise instructions for making something or to create an atmosphere as in a poem or a story.

Inaccurate spelling can interfere with communication
Inaccurate spelling can interrupt the flow of reading and make interpretation of the message less instant. Many people find it annoying enough to affect their attitude towards the writer. Major inaccuracies can even distort meaning.

There is an obvious conflict here. On the one hand the content of writing is more important than spelling. On the other, inaccurate spelling can hamper communication. Therefore, until accurate spelling of a very large number of words is mastered, writers are obliged to divide their attention between thinking about the content of their writing and deciding the order of the letters in each word.

Contrary to popular notion, there is a logical structure to spelling in the English language
The bases of words tend to be spelled consistently in whichever part of a word they appear, although they may be pronounced differently, e.g. 'sign' in 'resign' and 'signature'; 'one' in 'someone' and 'alone'. Recognising how words are constructed can prevent spelling errors in which letters are unnecessarily doubled or omitted. For example, knowing that adverbs are formed by adding 'ly' as in 'general(ly)', 'generous(ly)' should ensure that two 'l's are used in 'generally'.

Children develop an ability to isolate sounds in words and appear capable of learning letter–sound correspondences at an early age
Children can spell from an early age by matching the sounds they can hear in a word to the letters they have learned. For instance, a child who can hear all the sounds in the word 'giant' may write it 'jIunt'. Children whose ability to spell is based on the sounds they can hear in words develop phonemic awareness, which is also useful in learning to read.

Children appear to be able to learn kinaesthetically as well as visually
It is thought that children reinforce their learning of the spellings of words by rehearsing them in a connected handwriting style.

A further conflict exists here. If children are encouraged to use their developing ability to write words as they sound, they are very likely to misspell some words. Words which are written incorrectly a number of times could become learned motor patterns.

Children appear to be more motivated to learn and their learning is more durable and of a higher quality when they are actively involved in the learning and encouraged to make connections
Traditionally, spelling has been 'taught' only as a rote activity. Children's interest in words can be aroused, particularly if making meaningful connections between words takes the form of an investigation.

Taking these six, sometimes conflicting, points into consideration, what can be concluded about how to teach spelling in relation to writing? First of all we need to be clear that learning to spell is inextricably linked to, but not synonymous with, learning to write. Children's writing should not be hampered by the mechanics of spelling, but children must nevertheless learn how to spell. In practice this means that accurate spelling should not be expected when children are beginning to write. It would seem sensible to allow children to use the spelling strategy of hearing sounds in words at an early age. However, they should gradually be encouraged to use the correct spelling for words, particularly those which they use most often. As children become more proficient spellers and the spelling of words becomes automatic, their writing will be less hampered by the mechanics of spelling.

Although there is probably an element of motor practice in the learning of spelling, learning to spell, like all learning, should contain a major element of thinking. The English spelling system is by no means arbitrary, although there are occasions when it would appear so, particularly if one is looking for regularity of pronunciation. An obvious example is 'ough' ('bough', 'rough', 'though', 'through', 'thought'). On the other hand, many words which rhyme have a regular spelling pattern, e.g. 'light', 'might', 'tight', etc. In the early stages children can make useful connections at this level. Later, children can begin to see connections in meaning between words which contain the same pattern of letters, e.g. 'them', 'their', 'they'. Children should be encouraged to examine the order of letters in words and to make connections with other words. Building a cognitive framework of the language in this way is more likely to help children remember the spellings of words than rote learning a vast vocabulary of unrelated strings of letters.

LEARNING TO WRITE ▶

Given the opportunity, children engage in 'writing' as early as two and three years of age. This writing may consist of an imitation of an adult's cursive script or carefully designed symbols.

This early form of writing indicates that a child has begun to recognise that 'squiggles on a page' are designed to carry meaning.

Children's knowledge of the alphabet gradually becomes apparent in their writing, and they begin to connect sounds in the words to letters which they have learned 'make' a particular sound.

ix

Gradually they are able to hear other sounds in the words.

> Mis is nevol TolD The oleny groop That They coD go ind
>
> The wull grabru and we hat to Maes a Met. WiTh. sding.
>
> We cuT 7 Pesu of sding,
>
> We went a Wawlu BuT Frst We T.D The sting in a not. Wc went of. We PeT The string in a sooc and We caTD The Prnts.

Encouraging children to write using this developing ability serves two purposes.

1. It gives them more freedom to concentrate on the content of their writing than other methods such as asking the teacher for words or using a word bank. However, it cannot give total freedom because matching the sounds they can hear in words to 'correct' letters is laborious.
2. It develops their awareness of the sound structure of the language and their knowledge of the alphabetic system. This is an important part of the foundation of both reading and spelling.

As children become familiar with the conventions of the spelling system they will incorporate an increasing number of correctly spelled words into their writing. Their ability to spell words as they sound will still be useful as a temporary measure for new words. These would be amended in the final draft of the writing.

Not all composition needs to be written
It is important to emphasise that at all stages, but perhaps most particularly at the beginning, children should be given the opportunity to communicate or record without the added complication of spelling. Speaking to the class, a group, the teacher or other adult can be an alternative to writing. If recording is necessary, the teacher or other adult can act as scribe or a tape-recorder may be used. Older children could take turns at writing the results of a group investigation. Information can be recorded in other forms than continuous text, e.g. charts, graphs or pictures.

Learning to spell need not involve thinking about the content of the writing
Hearing sounds in words, learning letter shapes, looking at words, words within words, common letter-strings, common meanings, practising letter patterns and words, making up mnemonics and learning about language can be carried out as individual or group activities, games or investigations independently of story or report writing.

LEARNING TO SPELL

At the beginning, learning to spell consists of two elements:
a) learning to hear sounds in words
b) learning which letters of the alphabet generally correspond to these sounds.

Later, children will:
a) learn to examine the morphemic structure of words, which may not necessarily coincide with the phonemic (sound) structure

b) learn to spell common letter patterns
c) learn to spell a number of irregularly spelled words which occur frequently in their writing
d) learn spelling conventions.

This learning requires appropriate teaching and practice.

TEACHING SPELLING

In order to teach spelling, the teacher needs to know the children's existing capabilities. To a certain extent this can be assessed by examining the children's writing. However, for different reasons, children's writing does not always reflect their ability. At the beginning, children may not produce any writing at all. Further investigation may reveal that they cannot hear sounds in words although they have a reasonable knowledge of the alphabet. Conversely, they may be able to hear sounds in words but do not know which letters they match. Some children may have both facilities but may not have been encouraged to use them in order to write. They may only have been taught to copy underneath the teacher's writing.

If children have copied the teacher's writing it is obviously impossible to determine the extent of their spelling ability from that writing. Similarly, if children 'play safe' in their writing, using only those words they know how to spell, they will have no spelling errors in their piece of writing. However, the content of the writing will not necessarily reflect their knowledge or ability in terms of the subject matter. In this case the child's writing indicates an ability to make no spelling errors but not an ability to spell a wider range of words.

Additional forms of assessment would ensure that appropriate teaching strategies are adopted. This book offers assessments for children at different stages in spelling and suggestions for teaching based on the results of the assessments.

PART 1 BEGINNING TO SPELL

Given the opportunity children will spell by writing down the sounds they can hear in the words they want to say. In order to use this approach to spelling most effectively, children must be able to hear all the sounds in the words and have a thorough knowledge of letters. Research has shown that children generally learn to isolate the initial sound first (see example 1 below). In a monosyllabic word they will then learn the final sound (see example 2 below), and lastly the middle vowel.

Children can usually hear consonant blends more easily at the beginning rather than at the end of words.

Before embarking on a teaching programme to improve children's ability to hear sounds in words and their knowledge of letters, it is essential to know their present capabilities. The following chapters provide assessment material for this purpose and then suggestions and material for teaching those early skills.

1. *Kate is coming to my house tonight to play.*

2. *I like my toys and I like my gobot.*

ASSESSMENT

Children must be able to hear **sounds** in words and also know which **letters** to match to the sounds in order to start to spell.

It is important to assess both of these skills separately. If children are asked to write the letter which begins 'bat', they must not only be able to hear the first sound but also know the letter shape. Inability to respond correctly may be because they either cannot isolate the sound at the beginning of 'bat', or do not know which letter makes a 'b' sound, or both. An incorrect answer or lack of response to this question does not give us any information for teaching. This means that letters cannot be used to find out whether children can hear sounds in words. Similarly, words cannot be used to find out if a child knows the letters of the alphabet.

The first set of assessments in this chapter tests children's ability to hear the initial sound, the final sound, the medial sound and the consonant blends in words. The second set tests children's letter knowledge.

I usually carry out these assessments with a group of children. I prefer this to testing individually for two reasons. Firstly, I can keep one group in the class fully occupied while the rest of the children are busy with other activities. Secondly, there is the question of whether the children understand the task. While watching other children, a child may come to learn what is meant by 'saying the first sound of a word'. Testing a child individually means that numerous examples may be needed before the teacher can distinguish between a child who cannot hear the initial sound of a word and a child who does not understand the task. This can be unnecessarily time consuming.

SOUNDS

 C1–2

Assessment activity to find out if children can hear the initial sound in a word

Group size
Up to six children.

Equipment
1. Collection of about eight objects which begin with different sounds, such as:
- toy vehicles (car, van, motorbike, ambulance, fire engine, etc.).
- Fruit (apple, orange, peach, satsuma, kiwi fruit, etc.). Avoid objects such as grapes which start with a consonant blend and bananas in which the second syllable is stressed (children may say 'n' for 'nana').

2. List of the names of the children in the group for you to note down the results of the assessment.

Procedure
First demonstrate to the children what you mean by the 'first sound'. Their names are usually a good starting point. Then ask the children to tell you what sounds the objects on the table start with. Go round each child in turn, until you are satisfied that you know whether each child can hear the initial sound in a word.

Children who can hear the initial sound in a word can then be assessed to find out if they can hear the final sound in a word.

For children who cannot hear the initial sound see pages 4–5.

Assessment activity to find out if children can hear the final sound in a word

Group size
Up to six children.

Equipment
1. **Copymaster 1** with pictures of the following objects: pen, lid, bag, cup, jug, map, zip, dog, hen, cat, bus and van.
2. List of the names of the children in the group for you to note down the results of the assessment.

Procedure
Start by identifying the initial sound of each object and then explain that you are going to listen for final sounds. Follow similar procedure as for the previous assessment.

Children who can hear the final sound can go on to the next two assessments.

For suggestions for teaching those children who cannot hear the final sound see pages 9–10.

Assessment activity to find out if children can hear the middle vowel in a word

Group size
Up to six children.

Equipment
1. **Copymaster 1** with pictures of the following objects: pen, lid, bag, cup, jug, map, zip, dog, hen, cat, bus and van.

2. List of the names of the children in the group for you to note down the results of the assessment.

Procedure
Ask the children to tell you the initial and final sounds of one of the objects and then tell the children its middle vowel sound. Continue as in previous assessments.

Suggestions for teaching children who cannot hear the middle vowel in words are on pages 10–12.

Assessment activity to find out if children can hear initial and final consonant blends in words

Group size
Up to six children.

Equipment for initial blends
1. **Copymaster 2** with pictures of the following: brush, crab, clown, dress, flower, glove, grass, plate, stamp, smoke, skirt, sledge, snowman, spider, twenty.
2. List of the names of the children in the group for you to note down the results of the assessment.

Procedure
Establish that the children can hear the 'b' in 'brush' and then ask what comes after the 'b'. Repeat the procedure with all the pictures.

Equipment for final blends
1. A list of the following words: bend, sent, milk, lost, left, bump, sink.
2. List of the names of the children in the group for you to note down the results of the assessment.

Procedure
It is probably easier to ask the children for all the sounds in these words.

Suggestions for teaching children to hear consonant blends are on pages 12–13.

LETTERS

 C3–4

Assessment activity to find out if children know letters 's', 'm' and 'o', and 'p', 'f' and 'a'

Group size
Up to six children.

Equipment
Set of lower-case letters 's', 'm', 'o', 'p', 'f' and 'a' (plastic, wooden or written on card) for each child.

Procedure
Start with 's', 'm' and 'o'. Each child should put the three letters in a line. You say the sound of one of the letters, e.g. 'sss' as in sausage, 'mmm' as in mummy or 'o' as in orange, and the children should slide the correct letter into the middle of the table. (Don't say 's for snake', etc. since the children may only know the letters by visual connection with one picture.) To make sure that some children are not simply imitating the others you can vary the game by asking just two or three to play in some rounds. The same game can be played with the remaining three letters.

Assessment activity to find out if children know the remaining letters in the alphabet

Group size
Individual.

Equipment
Copymasters 3 and **4** stuck on to two pieces of A4 card. These are the test cards. Named sheet to note down results of assessment.

Procedure
Place one card in front of the child. Ask the child to point to the letter which you will say. Use the sounds of the letters and **don't** give an example of an object beginning with that letter because the child may only be able to identify that shape by association with that object – 'c' for 'cat', for instance.

Where possible the letter sounds should be held 'nnnnn', 'lllllll', 'zzzzzz', 'rrrrrrr', 'vvvvv'. Where this is not possible, e.g. 'b', 't', 'g', the least amount of extra vowel sound should be used. Avoid saying 'cuh', 'duh', etc.

Repeat procedure with the second card and record the letters which the child identifies.

Suggestions for teaching letters may be found on pages 5–8.

TEACHING BEGINNING SPELLING

This consists of teaching children to hear sounds in words and to recognise the letters of the alphabet.

Writing

If children are allowed to write using squiggles or letters to represent what they wish to say even though it bears no relationship to correct spelling, they can 'write' independently. When they write, they are likely to develop their spelling using the sounds they eventually learn to hear in words. Children need to be given the opportunity to write messages, lists, letters to a fictional character, to each other, to the teacher, instructions, stories, poems, reports, etc. Writing can be initiated by the teacher or by the children in their play. Children develop the ability to hear sounds in words with the express purpose of writing. This, however, is not necessarily an automatic transition. The connection between writing, hearing sounds and knowing letters needs to be made explicit.

Modelling early spelling in the process of writing

Group writing sessions can be used to show children how they can incorporate their spelling ability into their writing. For instance, the children could share in the writing of a report of an investigation they have just carried out. They dictate to the teacher, who writes in full view of the children on a white board or large piece of sugar paper. The teacher encourages the children to listen to the sounds in the words and say which sound comes next. It is highly likely that some of the words the children dictate will not conform to a strict sound–letter correspondence. Explain to the children that this is a problem with some words or odd parts of words and that they will eventually learn these words. Emphasise that they are learning to write and they should write the bits of the words which they can and that, gradually, they will learn to write more and more of the word correctly. At this stage children should not be made to feel dissatisfied with their own writing. However, children can see that their version of a word is different from the word printed in a book. We should not pretend that their versions are correct, but show that they are acceptable.

In order that children can start to write using sound–letter correspondence, they must learn to hear sounds in words and learn to recognise letter shapes. It is suggested that activities to develop both of these abilities take place side by side in an infant classroom.

HEARING INITIAL SOUNDS IN WORDS
C5–8, 15, 16, 18–21 ▶

Emphasise the initial sound of a word, e.g. 'sssssnake', 'mmmmmummy', 'ffffunfair', 'aaaapple' in which the initial sound can be continued, and 'ddddaddy' and 'pppppeter' in which the sounds can be repeated. Let the children watch and imitate your mouth.

Useful activities

● Play a very simply version of 'I spy'. Put three easily obtainable classroom objects which begin with different sounds (continuous) on the table in front of you, e.g. magnet, shell, ruler. After naming each object and exaggerating the initial sounds, the children and teacher can take turns at asking the others in the group to guess what they can spy.

The game can be made harder by:
a) using objects with initial sounds which cannot be sounded continuously, e.g. farm animals: cow, dog, pig, goat.
b) increasing the number of objects.

● Make a collection of objects starting with the same sound.
● Play 'My Grandmother went to market and she bought…' in which each child has to think up something beginning with the same letter.

● Make up funny sentences in which each word starts with the same letter, e.g. 'Small smoked sausages slide slowly into the stew'.

Pencil and paper activities: Copymasters 5–8

● **Copymaster 5** Put a circle round all the pictures which start with the same sound as the picture of the see-saw in the middle, as in the example shown.
● **Copymaster 6** Which of these children are doing something starting with 's' like the child in the middle? Put a cross by them, as in the example shown.
● **Copymaster 7** Odd-one-out. Put a circle round the picture in each line which starts with a different sound. The top line is given as an example.
● **Copymaster 8** Join a picture on one side of the page with the one on the other side which starts with the same sound, as in the example shown.

Pairs: game for up to four children

Preparation
Picture bank – stick the pictures from **Copymasters 15, 16, 18, 19, 20** and **21** on to small cards.

Activity
Choose 16 pictures, four starting with each of four sounds, e.g. finger, farm, fish, flute; doctor, duck,

4

dominoes, dress; six, signal, square, slippers; crocodile, cucumber, carriage, clouds. Spread the pictures out face down on the table. The first player turns two cards over. If they start with the same sound the child keeps that pair and turns over two more cards. That player's turn finishes when he/she turns two cards which do not have the same sound. These cards are turned face down again. The players try to remember the pictures on the cards which they have seen turned over. The second player turns a card over and then another. Play continues until all the cards have been paired. The winner is the player with the most pairs.

The game can be varied by using just two cards of each sound, and/or more sounds.

Snap: game for two to four children

Preparation
Picture bank – stick the pictures from **Copymasters 15, 16, 18, 19, 20** and **21** on to small cards.

Activity
Choose 16 pictures, four starting with each of four sounds, e.g. finger, farm, fish, flute; doctor, duck, dominoes, dress; six, signal, square, slippers; crocodile, cucumber, carriage, clouds. Deal out cards to players. Cards should be held in a pile, face down. The first player places his/her top card face up on the table in front of him/her.

The next player also places his/her top card on the table face up. When any two cards start with the same sound, the first player to shout 'snap' claims those cards and all the others underneath. Play continues until all the cards are held by one player. Alternatively, you can

play for a specified length of time and the winner is the player with the most cards.

The game can be varied by using just two cards of each sound, and/or more sounds.

Donkey: game for two to four children

Preparation
Picture bank – stick the pictures from **Copymasters 15, 16, 18, 19, 20** and **21** on to small cards.

Activity
Choose 16 pictures, four starting with each of four sounds, e.g. finger, farm, fish, flute; doctor, duck, dominoes, dress; six, signal, square, slippers; crocodile, cucumber, carriage, clouds. The dealer removes one card from the pack without looking at it, and hides it. The dealer deals out the cards. The players look at their cards. If two cards in their hand start with the same sound they show these to the other players and then discard them in the centre of the table. Players then fan their cards and hold them so that they cannot be seen by other players. The first player holds out his/her fan to the second player who chooses one card. If that card can be paired up with a card in the second player's hand, he/she again shows the pair to the other players and then discards it in the centre of the table. He/she then hold his/her fan for the next player to choose from. This process is continued round the table until a player is left with one card. The hidden card is then produced and should pair with that remaining card.

The game can be varied by using just two cards of each sound, and/or more sounds.

LETTERS

C9–35

c o a d g e f s (qu)

It is obviously not possible to teach all the letters at once. I teach letter recognition, letter formation and the sounds of letters at the same time so it is logical to group the letters according to their formation. For right-handed children the anticlockwise movement in the letter 'c' and all similarly formed letters ('o', 'a', 'd', 'g', 'q', 'e', 's', 'f') is unnatural; the scribbling movement usually being in the other direction. A lot of practice is therefore needed on these letters. Research has shown that children tend to get to know letters 's', 'a', 'f', and 'o' earlier than most other letters. For these reasons the 'c' group of letters is presented first here.

I give the letters characters according to their shapes and sounds and then concoct a story around them. For instance 'c' could be a 'curled-up cat' or a 'caterpillar'. It is important to emphasise the 'curled head'. This makes joining for 'o', 'a', 'd' and 'g' easier; there is less likelihood of leaving a gap, e.g. g/g. Plenty of gross motor practice is important. The children could paint different coloured 'caterpillars' with single strokes on to

large paper or move their finger round a large 'c' made out of sandpaper.

Pencil and paper activities: Copymasters 9–10
Copymaster 9 Join the letter on one side of the page with the identical letter on the other side, as in the example shown.
Copymaster 10 Join the pictures to the correct letter, as in the examples shown.

Sorting pictures I

Preparation
Stick the pictures from **Copymaster 11** on to small cards. To make the baseboards, you will need three pieces of A4 card. Take the pictures of the dog, cracker and fishing rod and stick one in the centre of each of the baseboards.

Activity
Children should sort out the pictures according to their initial letter and place them on the baseboard with the picture beginning with the same letter.

Sorting pictures II

Copymasters **15** and **16** contain a series of pictures with the initial letters 'c', 'o', 'a', 'd', 'g', 'e', 'f', 's':

grass	footprints	escalator	octopus
gloves	fish	envelope	orange
garden	farm	engine	guitar
gate	finger	elbow	goose
girl	flute	egg	doctor
grapes	forty	elephant	duck

dominoes	scarecrow	astronaut	carriage
dolphin	six	apple	cauldron
dress	signal	ambulance	cannon
diamond	square	ant	clouds
dragon	sausage	axe	crocodile
door	slippers	anchor	cucumber

Preparation
Letter bank – stick the appropriate letters from **Copymasters 12** and **13** on to small cards.
Baseboard – stick **Copymaster 14** on to a piece of A4 card.
Picture bank – stick the pictures from **Copymasters 15** and **16** on to small cards.

Place two of the cards from the letter bank in the top two spaces on the baseboard. Sort the pictures which begin with these letters and then shuffle them.

Activity
The children should place the pictures in the spaces on the baseboard below the correct letter. More than one baseboard can be made and a number of children can do this activity at the same time, using different pictures.

Pairs, snap and donkey with letters

Preparation
Letter bank – make two copies of each of **Copymasters 12** and **13** and stick the letters on to small cards.

Activity
Make up a pack of two of each of the following letters: 'c', 'o', 'a', 'd', 'g', 'e', 'f', and 's'.

See pages 4–5 for instructions for playing. In these games letters (rather than pictures) will be paired.

Pairs, snap and donkey with letters and pictures

Preparation
Letter bank – make two copies each of **Copymasters 12** and **13** and stick the letters on to small cards.
Picture bank – stick the pictures from **Copymasters 15** and **16** on to small cards.

Activity
Make up a pack of two of each of the following letters: 'c', 'd', 'e', and 'f' and two pictures starting with each of the same letters.

See pages 4–5 for instructions for playing. In these games a letter should be paired with a picture. The games can be played with more/different letters and pictures.

Lotto: game for up to four players and one caller

Preparation
Picture bank – stick the pictures from **Copymasters 15** and **16** on to small cards.

Cut two pieces of A4 card in half. Using letters from the letter bank (**Copymasters 12** and **13**) make four lotto cards:

1) dsa	2) oeg	3) cog	4) dec
efc	dsa	saf	gfo

Activity
One child has the pack of picture cards and is the caller. The other children each have a Lotto card. The caller shows a picture card to the players. The players work out the first sound of the picture and see if they have the corresponding letter on their Lotto boards. The first child to do so receives the card and places it over the letter on their board. The winner is the first to cover all their letters.

Initial letter dominoes: game for up to four children

Preparation
Stick the dominoes from **Copymaster 17** on to small cards.

Activity
Place dominoes upside-down on the table. Each player chooses six dominoes. Any remaining dominoes are placed at the edge of the table. The children take it in turns to start to play. The first player puts a domino face up in the centre of the table. Player 2 should place a letter next to a picture which starts with that letter or a picture next to a corresponding letter. If he/she does not have a domino with an appropriate letter or picture, he misses a turn and takes a spare domino, if there are any. The first player to finish his/her dominoes is the winner.

Pictures and letters from the picture and letter banks can be used to make further sets of dominoes.

b p r n m h k l t j i u w y v z sh ch th ▷

There are a number of ways in which these letters can be grouped. 'b', 'p', 'r', 'n', 'm', 'h' and 'k' are often grouped together because there are similarities in formation: the pen goes back up the original down stroke. The digraphs 'sh', 'ch' and 'th' should be learned at the same time as the individual letters.

Pencil and paper activity
Photocopy pictures from the picture bank (**Copymasters 18, 19, 20** and **21**) and letters from the letter bank (**Copymasters 12–13**). Make up worksheets with pictures down one side and letters down the other. Photocopy as required.

Ask the children to draw a line between each picture and its correct initial letter.

● **Copymasters 18, 19, 20** and **21** contain a series of pictures with the initial letters 'b', 'p', 'r', 'n', 'm', 'h', 'k', 'l', 't', 'j', 'i', 'u', 'w', 'y', 'v', 'z', 'sh', 'ch' and 'th':

thermometer	Mickey Mouse	Robin Hood	headphones
thimble	magnet	radio	hopscotch
thirty	monkey	rose	hosepipe
thumb	moon	rocket	hammer

three	motor bike	rabbit	horse
thorns	mouth	rake	helmet
broomstick	jacket	needle	shed
baby	jam	nettle	sheep
beehives	jigsaw	notes	sheets
Big Ben	jar	numbers	shell
biscuits	jelly	newspaper	shoes
bread	jewels	necklace	shelves
chair	video camera	umbrella	yacht
chain	van	up	yoyo
cherries	vest	under	zebra
cheese	violin	ink	zigzag
chick	volcano	igloo	upside down
church	vase	insect	Indian
television	petrol pump	walking stick	lawnmower
triangle	penny	wheel	ladybird
trumpet	piano	wigwam	lorry
typewriter	policeman	wheelbarrow	lightning
telephone	puppet	whistle	lightbulb
teapot	pirate	wellingtons	lighthouse

Pairs, snap and donkey with letters

Preparation
Letter bank – make two copies each of **Copymasters 12** and **13** and stick the letters on to small cards.

Activity
Make up a pack of two of each of the following letters: 'm', 'b', 'i', 't', 'r', 'h', 'sh' and 'u'.

See pages 4–5 for instructions for playing. In these games letters (rather than pictures) will be paired.

Another pack can be made up to practise the following letters: 'th', 'n', 'l', 'ch', 'v', 'z', 'p' and 'w'.

Pairs, snap and donkey with letters and pictures

Preparation
Letter bank – make two copies each of **Copymasters 12** and **13** and stick the letters on to small cards.
Picture bank – stick the pictures from **Copymasters 18, 19, 20** and **21** on to small cards.

Activity
Make up a pack of two of each of the following letters: 'm', 'b', 'i' and 't' and two pictures starting with each of the same letters.

See pages 4–5 for instructions for playing. In these games a letter should be paired with a picture.

The games can be played with more/different letters and pictures.

Pencil and paper activities

The picture bank (**Copymasters 18, 19, 20** and **21**) and letter bank (**Copymasters 12** and **13**) can be used to make more worksheets using this format. Letters which are sometimes confused, e.g. 'b'/'d', and sounds, e.g. 'e'/'i', can be practised using these worksheets.

- **Copymaster 22** Write 'sh' or 'ch' under each picture, as in the example given.

- **Copymaster 28** Write the correct initial letter under the pictures, as in the example given.
- **Copymaster 29** Put a circle round the correct initial letter under the pictures, as in the example given.
- **Copymaster 30** Put a circle round the correct initial letter beside the pictures, as in the example given.

Track game for two to four children

Preparation
Stick the track from **Copymasters 23** and **24** on to card. The children will also need one dice and one coloured counter each.

Activity
The first player throws the dice and moves the number of squares shown on the dice. If he/she lands on a letter, he/she moves to the picture which starts with that letter. If the player lands on a picture, he/she must move to the initial letter of that picture. Either of these options may require moving forward or backward. The first player to reach the finish is the winner.

More track games can be made by sticking pictures from **Copymasters 15, 16, 18, 19, 20** and **21** and letters from **Copymasters 12** and **13** on to track **Copymasters 40** and **41**.

Lotto: game for up to four players and one caller

Preparation
Picture bank – choose two pictures from the picture bank (**Copymasters 18, 19, 20** and **21**) for each of the following initial sounds 'w', 'b', 'i', 'm', 'p', 't', 'u', 'h', 'l', 'n', 'r', 'v', 'j', 'th', 'sh' and 'ch'.
Baseboards – stick **Copymasters 25** and **26** on to pieces of A4 card. Cut each sheet in half to make a total of four Lotto cards.

Activity
Play as on page 6.

Initial letter dominoes: game for up to four children

Preparation
Stick the dominoes from **Copymaster 27** on to small cards.

Activity
Play as on page 6.

Animal letters: game for three players and one caller

Preparation
Stick the following letters from **Copymasters 12** and **13** on to small cards: 'f', 'l', 's', 'a', 'b', 'w', 'k', 'm', 'e', 'h', 'o', 'z', 'r', 'g', 'd', 't', 'c' and 'p'. Stick baseboards (**Copymasters 31, 32** and **33**) on to pieces of A4 card.

Activity
The caller has the pack of letters. Each player has a baseboard. The caller shows a card. The players look on their baseboards for an animal or insect which starts with that letter. If they find one, they place the letter in a square on the baseboard. The winner is the first to collect six letters.

7

**Postboxes: individual or group activity
(distinguishing 'b'/'d')**

Preparation

You need two boxes (shoe boxes or larger). Place the
boxes upside down and cut slits in the side for
postboxes. Using the letters from the letter bank
(**Copymasters 12** and **13**), stick 'c', 'a' and 'd' on to one
box and 'l', 'h' and 'b' on the other, above the slit. Sort
the six pictures from the picture banks (**Copymasters
15, 16, 18, 19, 20** and **21**) which begin with the six
sounds 'c', 'a', 'd', 'l', 'h' and 'b', and shuffle them
– thirty-six pictures in all.

Checking boards – stick **Copymasters 34** and **35** on to
A4 card.

Activity

The children post the pictures into the postbox with the
correct initial letter.

When they have finished, they get the checking
boards. They match the pictures from one postbox with
those on one checking board and the pictures from the
other box with the other checking board.

RHYMING

The connection between an ability to rhyme and success
in learning to read and spell has been emphasised in a
number of research studies. Children's first
introduction to rhyming is usually through nursery
rhymes, traditional or modern. There are a great many
books of rhymes and songs, as well as books which tell
stories in rhyme. Some of these are listed on page 9.
Learning some rhymes off by heart is a first stage;
number rhymes are particularly good as they serve a
dual purpose. Then children can be encouraged to make
up their own rhymes.

Useful activities

●   Clapping and skipping rhymes can be encouraged
in the playground.
●   Rhyme and rhythm are natural partners. Children
enjoy making up nonsense rhymes. It is a good idea to
start them off with a couplet to which they can add
different endings, e.g.:

> Mrs Plunket's in the bin,
> She's looking for a (drawing pin)
> (baked bean tin)
> (double chin)

●   Familiar rhymes can have one word changed and
the children change the rest to fit, e.g.:

> Mary had a little pig,
> Its hide was pink and black
> It followed her to school one day
> And promptly was sent back.

> Mary had a little cow,
> Its coat was brown and white
> It followed her to school one day
> etc. …

●   Once children are familiar with a number of
limericks they can change the words at the ends of the
lines, or even start making up their own.
●   Children can continue to add more couplets to
rhymes such as *Each peach, pear, plum* (Ahlberg).
●   Ask the children to make a collection of things that
rhyme.
●   The children can find as many things as they can
which rhyme with their names.

Generally, rhyming activities are best done in a class or
group where rhythm is incorporated and a sense of the
ridiculous often pervades. For quieter moments some
activities are suggested below.

Copymasters 36 and **37** are a series of rhyming pictures:

gate – plate	man – pan
goat – coat	mop – top
hair – chair	cat – hat
stair – pear	four – door
bear – square	sandal – candle
cake – rake	moon – spoon
parrot – carrot	mouse – house
bricks – six	frog – dog
star – car	fox – box
soap – rope	sock – clock
honey – money	key – tree
hen – pen	chips – whips

These pictures can be used for the following activities:

Sorting activities

Preparation

Picture bank – stick the pictures from **Copymasters 36**
and **37** on to small cards.

Activity

The pictures from the two copymasters should be kept
separate for this activity. First, using **Copymaster 36**,
the children can sort the pictures into rhyming pairs.
(They may spot the group of six pictures which rhyme.)

The pictures in **Copymaster 37** can be sorted in the
same way.

Pairs, snap and donkey

Preparation

Picture bank – stick the pictures from **Copymasters 36**
and **37** on to small cards.

Activity

At the beginning limit the rhyming pairs to just six, e.g.
mop – top, cat – hat, four – floor, sandal – candle, moon
– spoon, mouse – house.

See pages 4–5 for instructions for playing. In these
games rhyming pictures will be paired. The games can
then be played with more/different pictures.

Pencil and paper activities: Copymasters 38 and 39

- **Copymaster 38** In each row find the small picture which rhymes with the large picture on the left. Put a cross by it, as in the example given.
- **Copymaster 39** In each row find the small picture which rhymes with the large picture on the left. Put a cross by it, as in the example given.

Track game for two to four children

Preparation
Stick pictures of rhyming pairs from **Copymasters 36** or **37** on to a track. (Use the track **Copymasters 40–41**).

Activity
See page 7 for instructions. When the child lands on a picture, he/she has to move to the rhyming pair, whether it be forwards or backwards.

Suggested rhyming books

Inky Pinky Ponky	Michael Rosen and Susanna Steel	Picture Lions
Did I ever tell you how lucky you are?	Dr Seuss	A Dr Seuss Paperback Classic
Green eggs and ham	Dr Seuss	Beginner Books
Hop on Pop	Dr Seuss	Beginner Books
Singing in the sun	Jill Bennett	A young Puffin
Poems for the seven year olds and under	Helen Nicoll	A young Puffin
Along the line	Bernard Cribbins	A Macdonald book
A grand band	John Burningham	Walker
Bears in pairs	Niki Yektai	Viking Kestrel
Find me a tiger	Lynley Dodd	Puffin
The nickle nackle tree	Lynley Dodd	Picture Puffin
A dragon in a wagon	Lynley Dodd	Picture Puffin
Hairy Maclary	Lynley Dodd	Spindlewood
The fish who could wish	John Bush and Corky Paul	OUP
Mother Goose comes to Cable St.	Rosemary Stones and Andrew Mann	Picture Puffin
The park in the dark	Martin Waddell and Barbara Firth	Walker
Mister Magnolia	Quentin Blake	Picture Lions
All join in	Quentin Blake	Red Fox
Nursery rhyme book	Quentin Blake	Picture Lions
Peepo	Janet and Alan Ahlberg	Picture Puffins
Each peach, pear, plum	Janet and Alan Ahlberg	Picture Lions
Mother Goose	Brian Wildsmith	Oxford
Kids	Catherine and Laurence Anholt	Walker
Quacky quack-quack	Ian Whybrow and Russell Ayto	Walker
Ten, nine, eight	Molly Bang	Picture Puffins
Dancing and singing games	Pie Corbett and Sally Emerson	Kingfisher
Action rhymes	Sally Emerson and Pie Corbett	Kingfisher
Playtime rhymes	Pie Corbett	Kingfisher
Eeny meeny miny mo	Pie Corbett	Kingfisher
Clapping rhymes	Pie Corbett	Kingfisher
Skipping rhymes	Pie Corbett	Kingfisher

HEARING FINAL SOUNDS IN WORDS

C42 –53

Once children are good at isolating the initial sound in a word, they should be encouraged to hear the final sound. The approach taken can be similar to that for initial sounds (see pages 4–5).
   Some objects to use:

   classroom and home-corner: ball, pen, book, cup, knife, plate;

   from the farm: pig, dog, hen, cat, goat, horse, sheep;

   clothes: skirt, shirt, blouse, trousers, dress, sock, shoe (ends in 'oo' sound), ribbon, slide, clip.

Copymasters 42 and **43** contain a series of pictures ending in: 'k', 'd', 'ge', 'ing', 'l', 's', 't', 'n' and can also be used.

book	fork	sack	sock	hook	brick
bed	bird	bread	ladybird	shed	spade
bridge	cabbage	orange	sledge	cage	bandage
ring	wing	king	swing	spring	skipping
snail	shell	wheel	doll	bell	ball
horse	house	purse	bus	mouse	goose
pan	pen	sun	van	crown	train
cat	goat	kite	gate	hat	boat

Sorting pictures I

Preparation
Stick the pictures from **Copymasters 42** and **43** on to small cards.
   Make three baseboards by sticking copies of

9

Copymaster 44 on to pieces of A4 card. Sort the six pictures which end in 's', 'ing', and 'ge'. Put one of the pictures ending in 's' on a square on one baseboard, a picture ending in 'ing' on another baseboard, and a picture ending in 'ge' on the third baseboard.

Activity
Children should sort the pictures according to their final letter and place them on the baseboard which has the picture ending with the same letter.

This can be varied using different combinations of pictures.

Pairs, snap and donkey with pictures

Preparation
Picture bank – stick the pictures from **Copymasters 42** and **43** on to small cards. Make up a pack of two pictures of each of the final sounds.

Activity
See pages 4–5 for instructions for playing.

Further games of snap and pairs can be played with four of each of the pictures.

Pencil and paper activities: Copymasters 45 and 46

● **Copymaster 45** Put a circle round the picture which is the odd-one-out, as in the example given (i.e. ends with a different sound from the others in the row).
● **Copymaster 46** Put a cross by all the pictures which end with an 'l' sound, as in the example given.

Beginning and ending dominoes: an activity or game for one to four children

Preparation
Stick pictures from **Copymaster 47** on to small cards.

Activity
The procedure is similar to that for initial letter dominoes on page 6, but in this activity the final sound of one picture should be matched with the initial sound of the next picture and so on, e.g. flag–grass–stamp–postcard, etc. It need not be played as a game but just as an individual or group activity to make a long snake of words.

Sorting pictures II – using letters

Preparation
Letter bank – stick the letters 'k' and 'n' from **Copymasters 12** and **13** on to small cards.

Baseboard – stick **Copymaster 14** on to a piece of A4 card.
Picture bank – stick the pictures from **Copymasters 42** and **43** on to small cards. Place the letters 'k' and 'n' in the top two spaces on the baseboard. Sort the pictures which end with these letters and then shuffle them.

Activity
The children should place the pictures in the spaces on the baseboard below the letters.

Track game for two to four children

Preparation
Stick pictures from **Copymasters 42** and **43**, and letters from **Copymasters 12** and **13** on to the track **Copymasters 40–41**.

Activity
See page 7 for instructions. When the child lands on a picture, he/she has to move to the corresponding final letter, whether it be forwards or backwards. If he/she lands on a letter he/she moves to a picture which ends with that letter.

Pencil and paper activities using letters

● **Copymaster 48** Join the pictures to the correct letter, as in the examples given.
● **Copymaster 49** Write the correct final letter in the box under each picture, as in the example given.
● **Copymaster 50** Join the pictures to the correct letter, as in the examples given. Children could use different colours for clarity.
● **Copymaster 51** Choose the correct word next to each picture and draw a circle round it, as in the example given.

Further worksheets can be made using the letters on **Copymasters 12** and **13** and the pictures on **Copymasters 42** and **43**.

Beginning-and-end letters: individual or group activity

Preparation
Stick the letters and pictures on **Copymasters 52** and **53** on to small cards and shuffle them.

Activity
Children should find the initial letter for each picture and place it in front of the picture and find the final letter and place it after the picture.

HEARING SHORT VOWELS IN WORDS

Similar procedures may be adopted for teaching children to hear a vowel in the middles of words as used for the initial and final sounds, see pages 4–10. I find children get the idea of the middle vowel when they imitate me opening my mouth wide and shouting!

Some objects to use from the farm: pig, dog, hen, cat.

Copymasters 54–56 contain a series of pictures containing the short vowels 'a', 'e', 'i', 'o', and 'u'.

a	e	i	o	u
cat	bed	bib	box	brush
flag	bell	fish	cock	bus
tap	desk	chips	dog	sun
van	dress	tin	doll	slug
hand	ten	witch	frog	nuts
hat	tent	whip	top	cup
bag	vest	king	lock	cub
jam	web	wing	log	drum
lamb	hen	pins	mop	duck
man	leg	pig	shop	thumb
map	peg	ring	socks	mug
mat	pen	six	clock	
pan	shed	swing	cross	
pram	shell	bridge		
sack	sledge	chicks		
stamp	men	hill		

Sorting pictures I

Preparation

Stick the pictures from **Copymasters 54, 55** and **56** on to small cards.

Make baseboards by sticking three copies of **Copymaster 44** on to pieces of A4 card. Sort six pictures with middle vowels 'a', 'o', and 'i'. Put one of the pictures with a middle vowel 'a' on a square on one baseboard, a picture with a middle vowel 'o' on another baseboard, and a picture with a middle vowel 'i' on a third baseboard.

Activity

Children should sort the pictures according to their middle vowel and place them on the baseboard with a picture beginning with the same letter.

This can be varied using different combinations of pictures.

Pairs, snap and donkey with pictures

Preparation

Picture bank – stick the pictures from **Copymasters 54, 55** and **56** on to small cards. Make up a pack of two pictures of each of the medial sounds.

Activity

See pages 4–5 for instructions for playing.

Further games of snap and pairs could be played with four or more of each of the pictures.

Pencil and paper activities: Copymasters 57 and 58

- **Copymaster 57** Join the pictures with 'o' in the middle with a blue line. Join the pictures with 'i' in the middle with a red line. Join the pictures with 'u' in the middle with a green line.
- **Copymaster 58** Start in the centre with the picture of the 'web'. Put a circle round all the pictures which have the same middle vowel as 'web'. The first one has been done.

Sorting pictures II – using letters

Preparation

Letter bank – stick the five vowels from **Copymasters 12** and **13** on to small cards.

Baseboard – stick **Copymaster 14** on to a piece of A4 card.

Picture bank – stick the pictures from **Copymasters 54, 55** and **56** on to small cards. Place the letters 'a' and 'i' in the top two spaces on the baseboard. Sort six of the pictures with these letters in the middle and then shuffle them.

Activity

The children should place the pictures in the spaces on the baseboard below the correct letters.

This activity should then be repeated with different vowels. The two which children tend to confuse the most are 'e' and 'i'.

Track game for two to four children

Preparation

Stick pictures from **Copymasters 54, 55** and **56**, and the vowels from **Copymasters 12** and **13** on to the track **Copymasters 40** and **41**.

Activity

See page 7 for instructions. When the child lands on a picture, he/she has to move to the corresponding middle vowel, whether it be forwards or backwards. If the player lands on a letter he/she moves to a picture which has that middle vowel.

Pencil and paper activities using letters: Copymasters 59–72

- **Copymaster 59** Put a circle round the correct word next to the pictures, as in the example given.
- **Copymasters 60** and **61** Using the letters at the top of the page, write the correct vowels in the middle of the words.
- **Copymaster 62** Draw a line from the pictures to the correct letter, as in the example given. Children could use a different colour for each vowel.
- **Copymaster 63** Circle the correct vowel for each picture, as in the example given.
- **Copymasters 64** and **65** Using the letters at the top of the copymaster, write the correct vowels in the middle of the words.
- **Copymasters 66** and **67** Using the letters at the top of the copymaster, write the words under the pictures as in the examples shown.
- **Copymaster 68** Fill in the crossword by writing in the names of the numbered pictures.
- **Copymasters 69** and **70** Look at the pictures on the left-hand side of the page. Join the picture to the correct letter-string in the middle of the page, then join it to the correct rhyming picture on the right-hand side of the page and then write the word under the picture, as in the example given.
- **Copymasters 71** and **72** Finish writing the words under the pictures.

Making rhyming words: individual or paired activity.

Preparation

Stick pictures from **Copymasters 54, 55** and **56,** and the letters from **Copymasters 12** and **13** on to small cards. Sort the following groups of pictures:

a) cat, mat, hat
b) ring, king, wing
c) ten, hen, men, pen
d) van, pan, man
e) mop, shop, top

and the following letters: 'a', 'o', 'e', 'i', 'c', 'n', 'r', 'k', 'w', 't', 'h', 'm', 'p', 'v', 'sh' and 'ng'.

Activity
Children should take one of the groups of pictures and make the word of one of the pictures using the letters. They should then count how many letters they need to change in order to make another word in the group.

LONG VOWELS

C73 –78

There are a number of alternative ways to spell each of the vowel sounds. However, some spellings occur more frequently than others. It is therefore worth teaching some of the more common vowel combinations, e.g. 'oo', 'ee', 'ai', 'ow'.

Three lotto games have been included to give some practice.

Lotto I ('ai', 'ow', 'ir', 'oo'): game for two to four players and a caller

Preparation
Stick the pictures from **Copymaster 73** on to small cards and shuffle them.

Stick **Copymaster 74** on to A4 card and cut it to make the four baseboards.

Activity
The caller shows a picture to the players who claim it if they have that word on their board. The winner is the first to collect all their five cards.

Lotto II ('ou', 'ea', 'oo', 'oa'): game for two to four players and a caller
As for Lotto I but using **copymasters 75** and **76**.

Lotto III ('ow', 'ar', 'or', 'ee'): game for two to four players and a caller
As for Lotto I but using **copymasters 77** and **78**.

HEARING CONSONANT BLENDS IN WORDS

C79– 88

Generally children can hear initial consonant blends once their attention has been drawn to them. Some children seem to need the visual aid of the letters. For children who experience difficulties, it is a good idea to make associations between the letter blends and pictures which have those blends at the beginning, e.g. 'st' for 'star' and 'tr' for 'train'. A difficult distinction is often between 'tr' and 'ch'. It is not unusual to see young children writing 'ch' or 'chr' for 'train'.

Final consonant blends are thought to be more difficult to hear than initial blends, particularly 'nd' and 'nt'. However, most children recognise the difference in meaning between 'wet' and 'went', 'bed' and 'bend', 'let' and 'lent', indicating that they can, in fact, hear the difference. This needs to be pointed out to them.

A 'st'-story: a class or group listening activity
Read the following story to the children. Ask them if they notice something peculiar about the sounds of many of the words. Read it again, a sentence at a time, and ask them how many 'st' sounds they can hear in each sentence.

I was strolling down West Street in Stockport on my way home for tea, when I saw a strange sight.
A man was standing quite still, on just one leg, as stiff and as steady as a stork.
He stayed like that for a few minutes and then started to stamp his feet hard.

I watched him pick up his stick, stumble, and then stagger down the street.
I went home and got stuck into the last plate of stew.

Similar stories can be made up around other blends.

Matching pictures to letter blends: an individual or group activity

Preparation
Stick the pictures from **Copymaster 79** on to small cards. Stick **Copymasters 80** and **81** on to A4-card.

Activity
The children should place the pictures on to the correct letter blend.

Sorting 's' blends: an individual or group activity

Preparation
Stick the pictures from **Copymaster 82** on to small cards. Stick **Copymaster 83** on to A4 card.

Activity
Pile the pictures on to the correct letter blend.

Score four: an individual activity

Preparation
Stick **Copymaster 84** on to A4 card.

Activity
Put your finger on START. Follow the arrow. Decide which letter blend is correct for the picture. Continue following the arrows. You will either return to START or get a score between 1 and 4.

Pencil and paper activities: Copymasters 85–88
- **Copymaster 85**   Using the letter blends at the top of the page, write the correct blend in each of the boxes.

- **Copymaster 86**   Write the second letter of the words in the spaces under the pictures, as in the example given.
- **Copymaster 87**   Put a ring round the correct word next to each picture, as in the example given.
- **Copymaster 88**   Write the correct word under each picture, as in the example given.

THE ALPHABET

Singing the alphabet seems to be a successful way of learning it. One common version is to the tune of 'Twinkle twinkle little star' with a slight variation at the end.

A   B   C   D   E   F   G   H   I   J   K   L   M   N   O   P

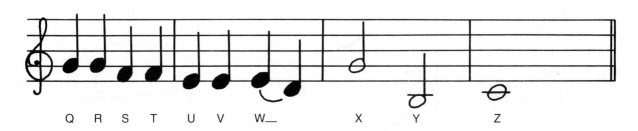

Q   R   S   T   U   V   W___   X   Y   Z

Children also enjoy dot-to-dot activities for practising the order of letters in the alphabet.

Dot-to-dot (lower case): Copymasters 89 and 90
Start at 'a' and join the dots in alphabetical order to make the shape.

Dot-to-dot (upper case): Copymasters 91 and 92
Start at 'A' and join the dots in alphabetical order to make the shape.

Matching upper- and lower-case letters: Copymaster 93
Draw a line between the upper- and lower-case letters, as in the example given.

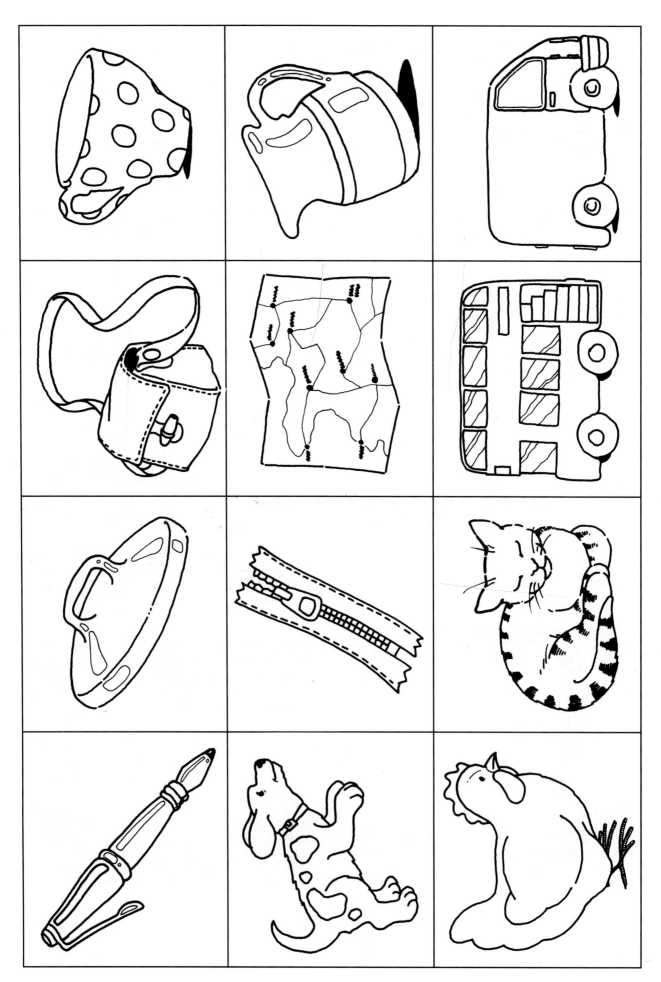

z

j

k

v

w

l

g

h

i t

y

t

c

n

e

qu

r

d

b

u

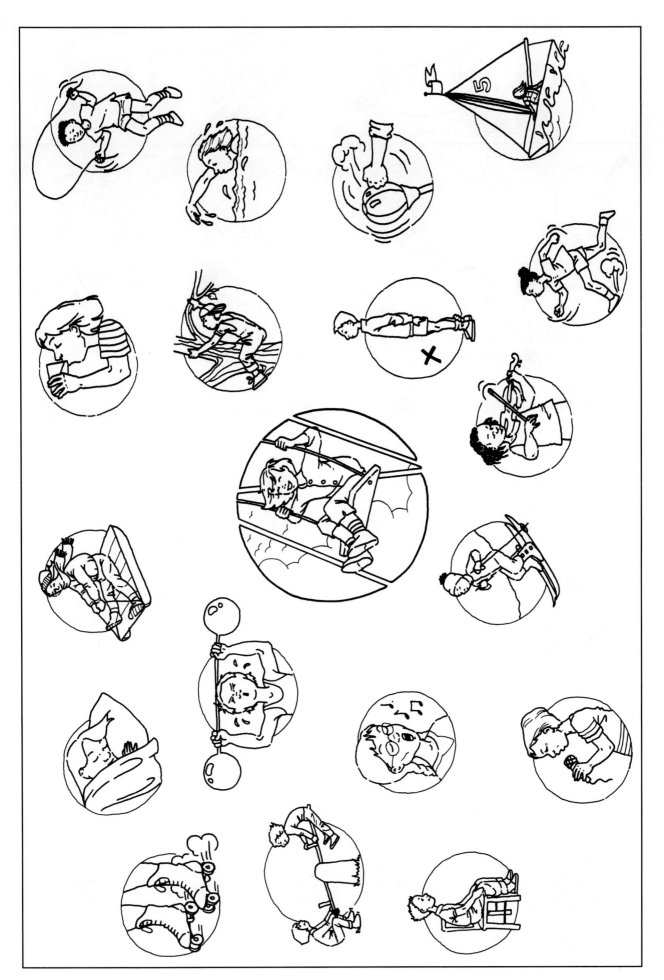

c   g

a   s

g   c

e   o

s   f

f   e

d   a

o   d

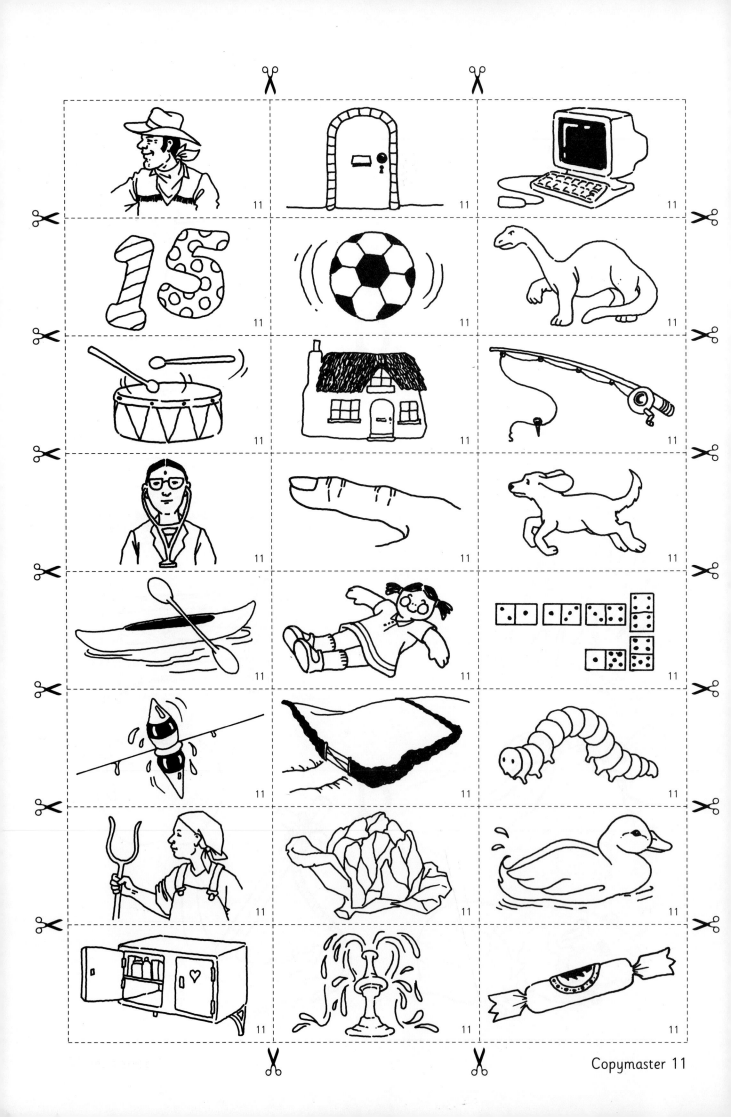

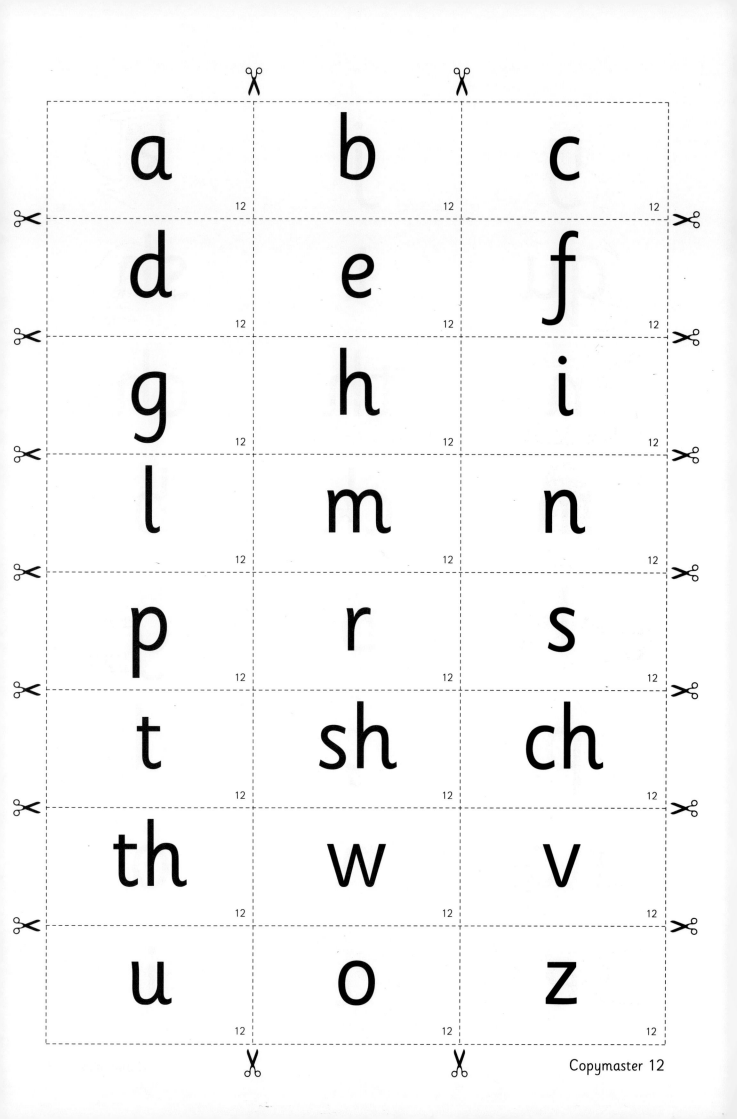

a	b	c
d	e	f
g	h	i
l	m	n
p	r	s
t	sh	ch
th	w	v
u	o	z

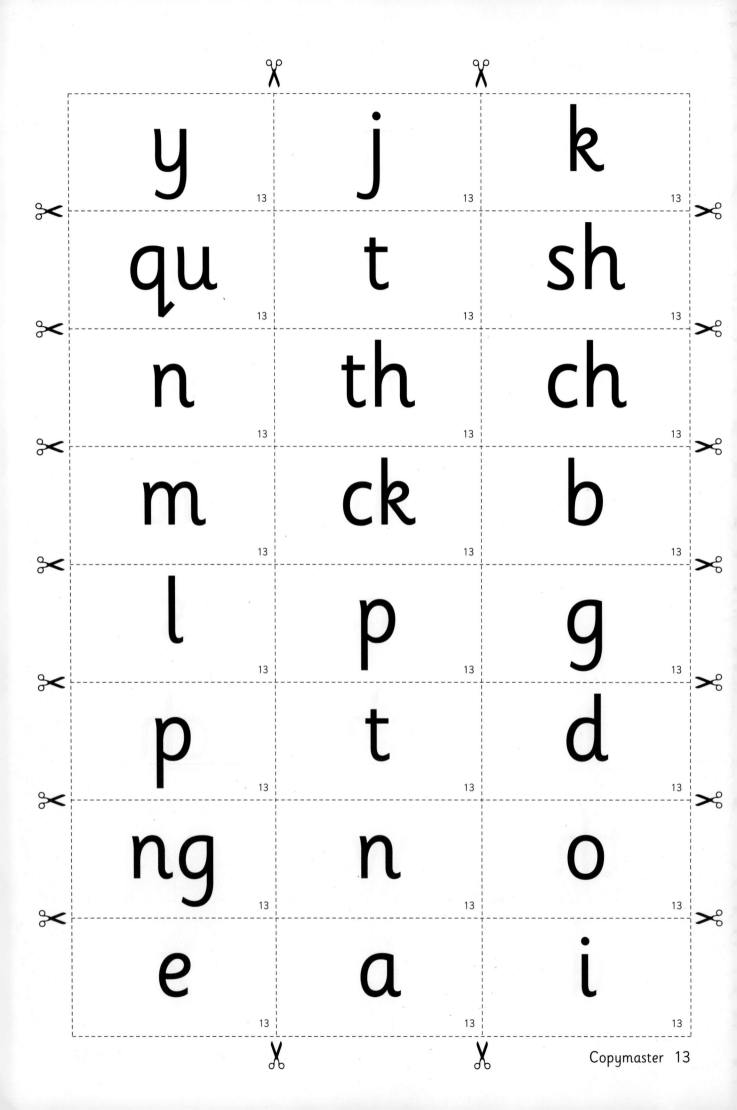

y	j	k
qu	t	sh
n	th	ch
m	ck	b
l	p	g
p	t	d
ng	n	o
e	a	i

Copymaster 15

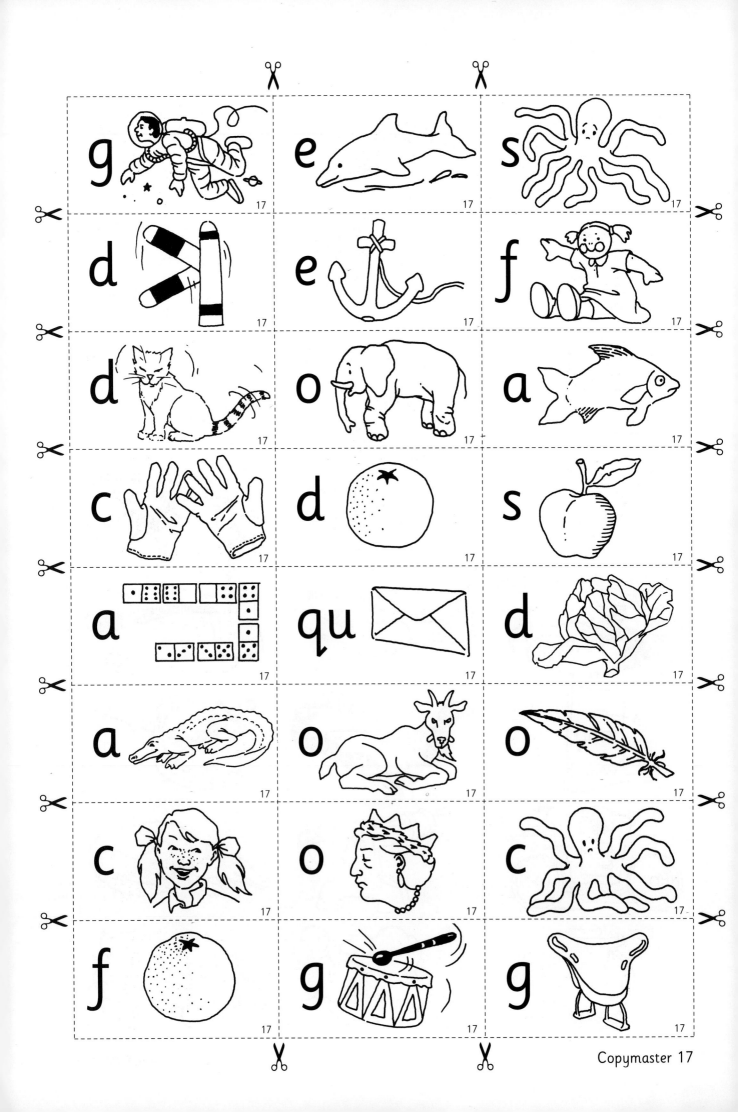

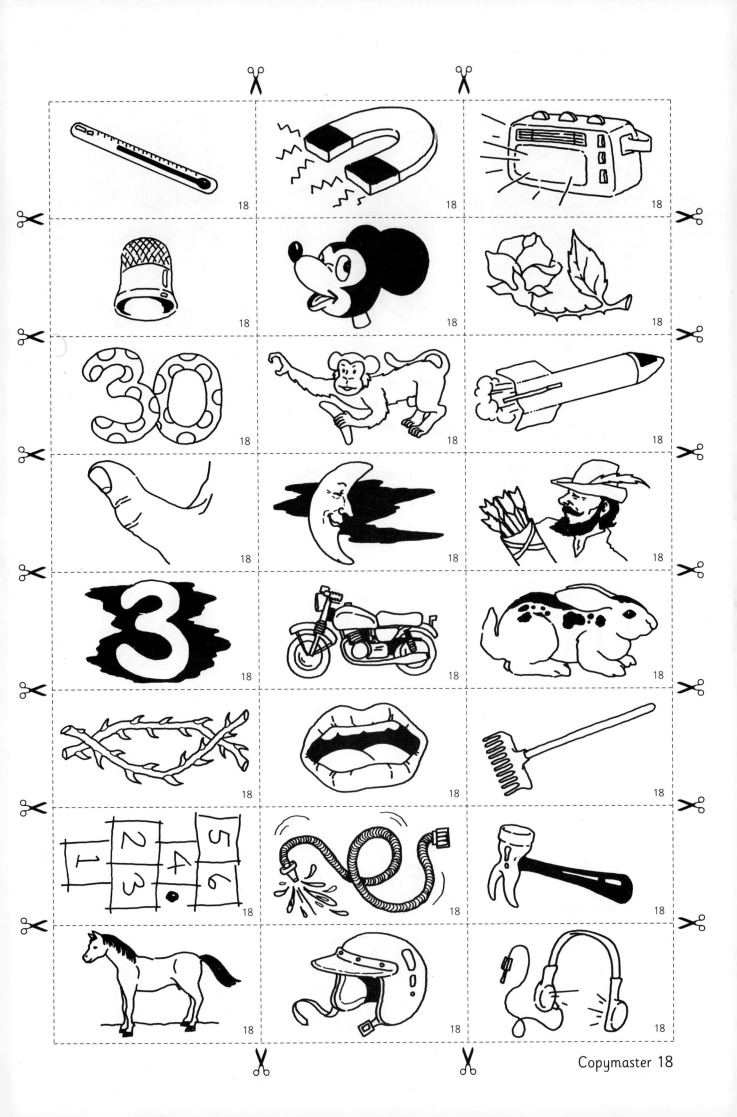

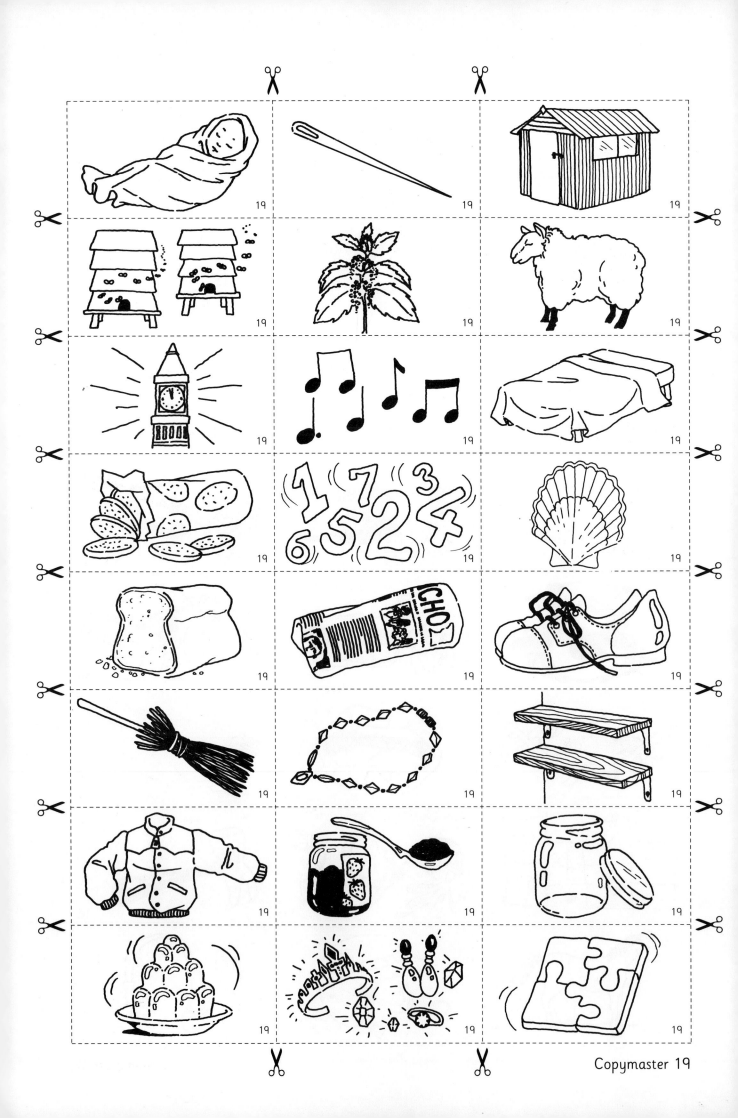

Copymaster 20

Copymaster 21

sh   ch

sh

Copymaster 22

w	b	i
m	p	th
u	sh	l
r	v	j

25

25

n	th	p
w	i	r

h	b	ch
m	t	j

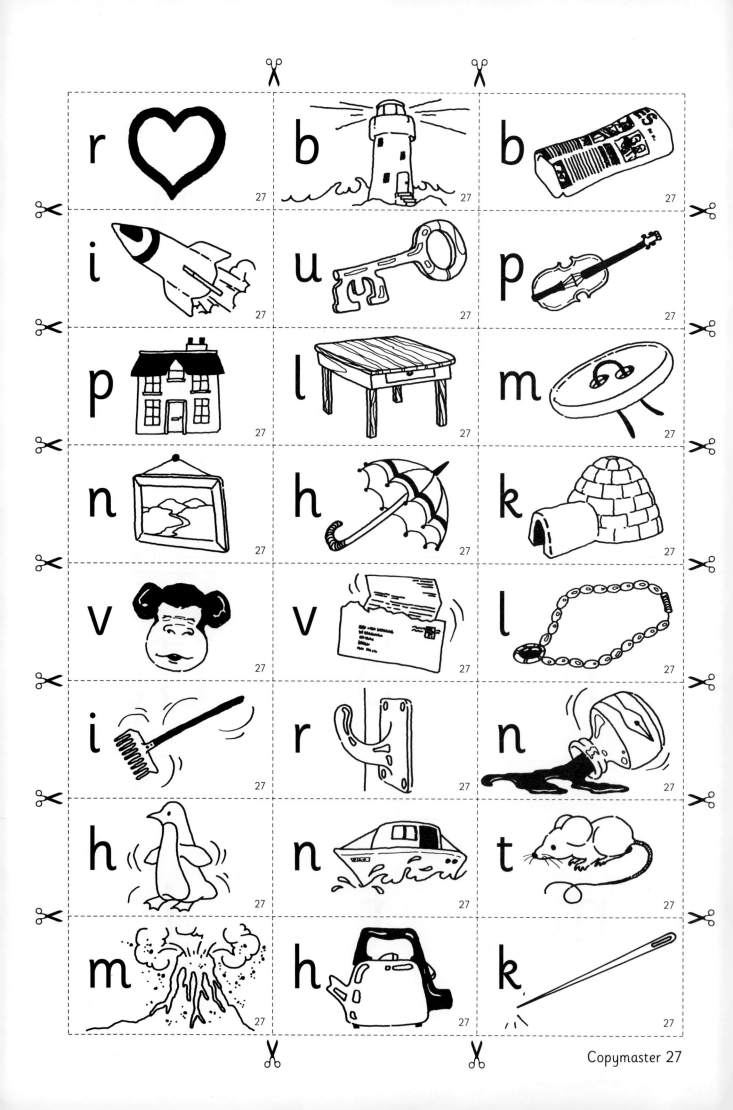

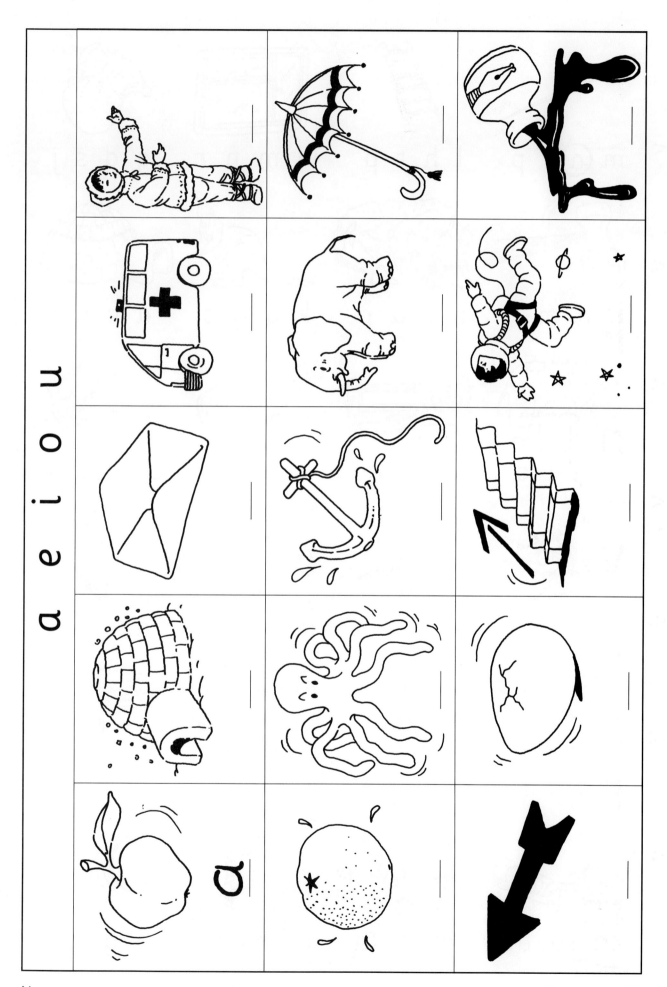

m (n) r p   l h t p   w m n r   g d s j

h n m r   n r d p   k g d s   a e i u

a e i o   j g p qu   t b k l   qu n t k

f g p t   m p t n   m r n w   a e i u

z c s a   v w x y   s m n z   h l t k

ch sh th   ch sh th   ch sh th   p g y j

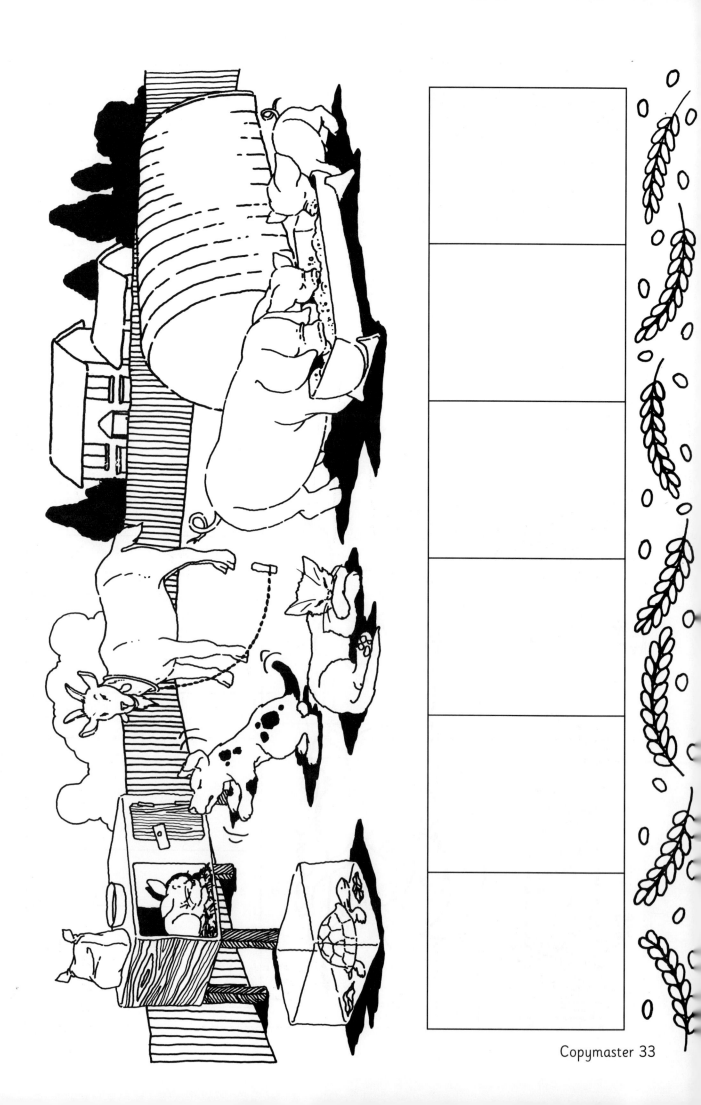

c a d

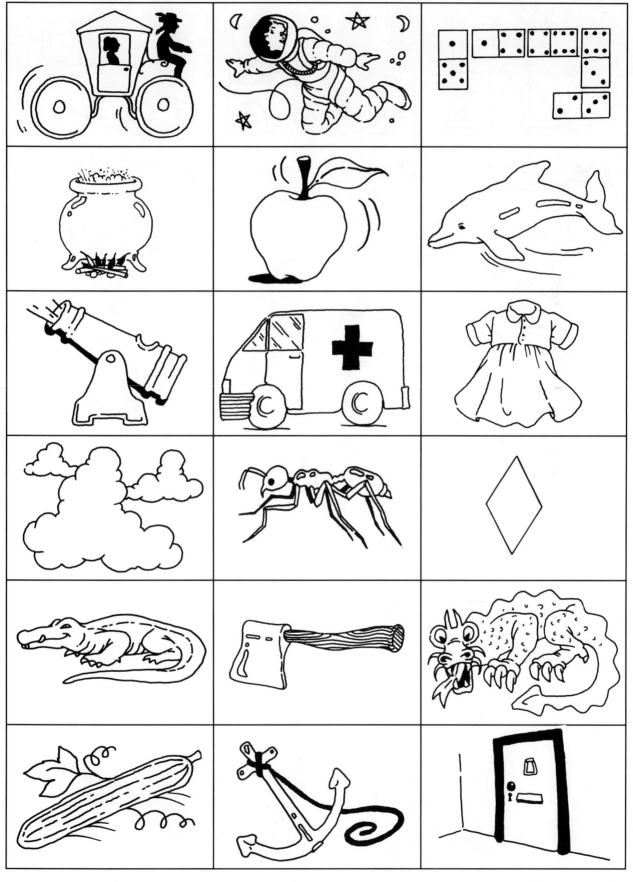

l h b

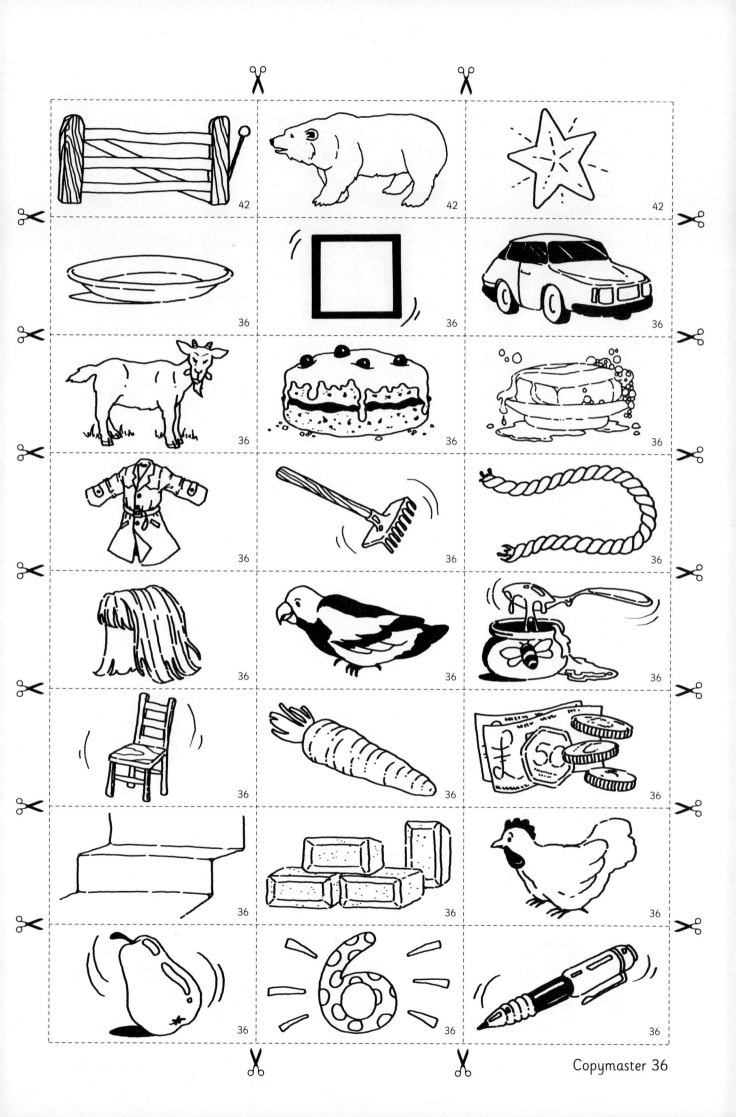

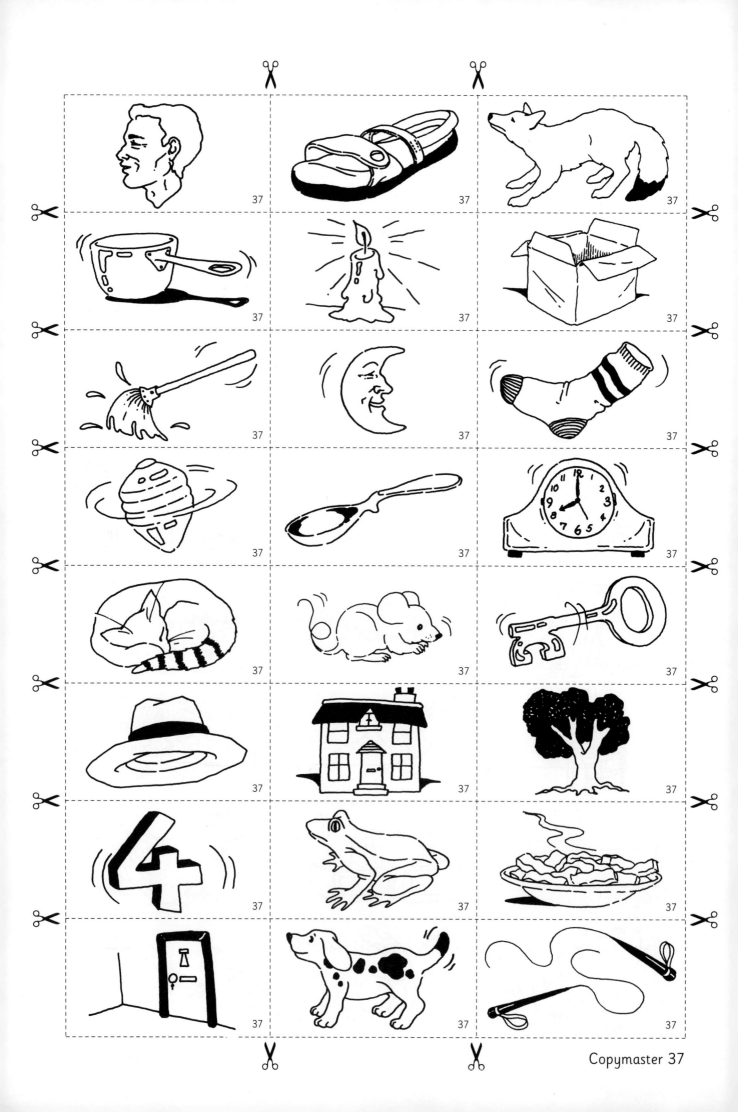

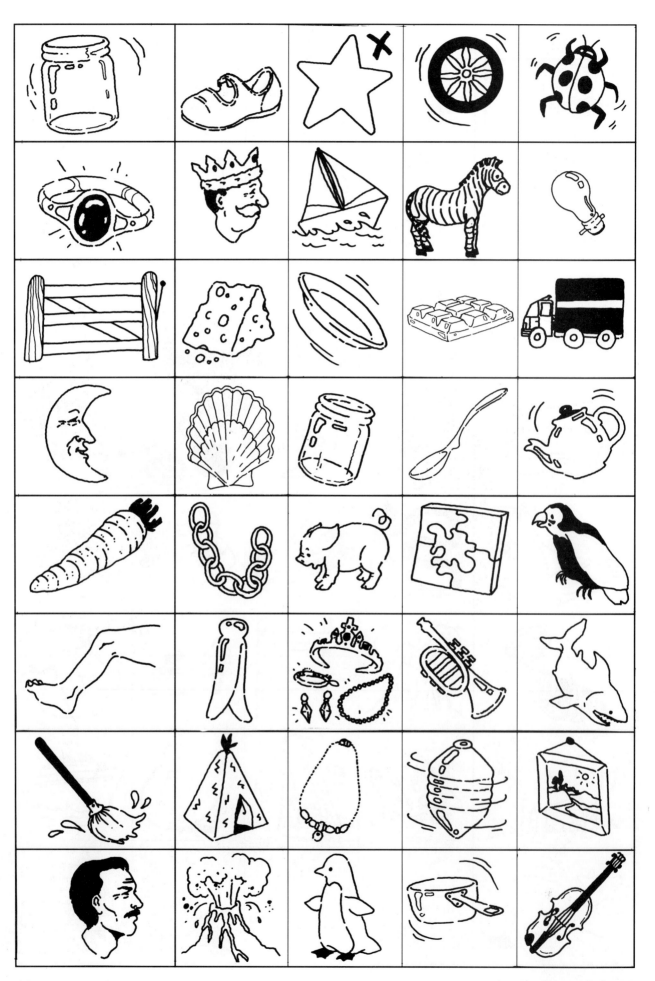

Start

Finish

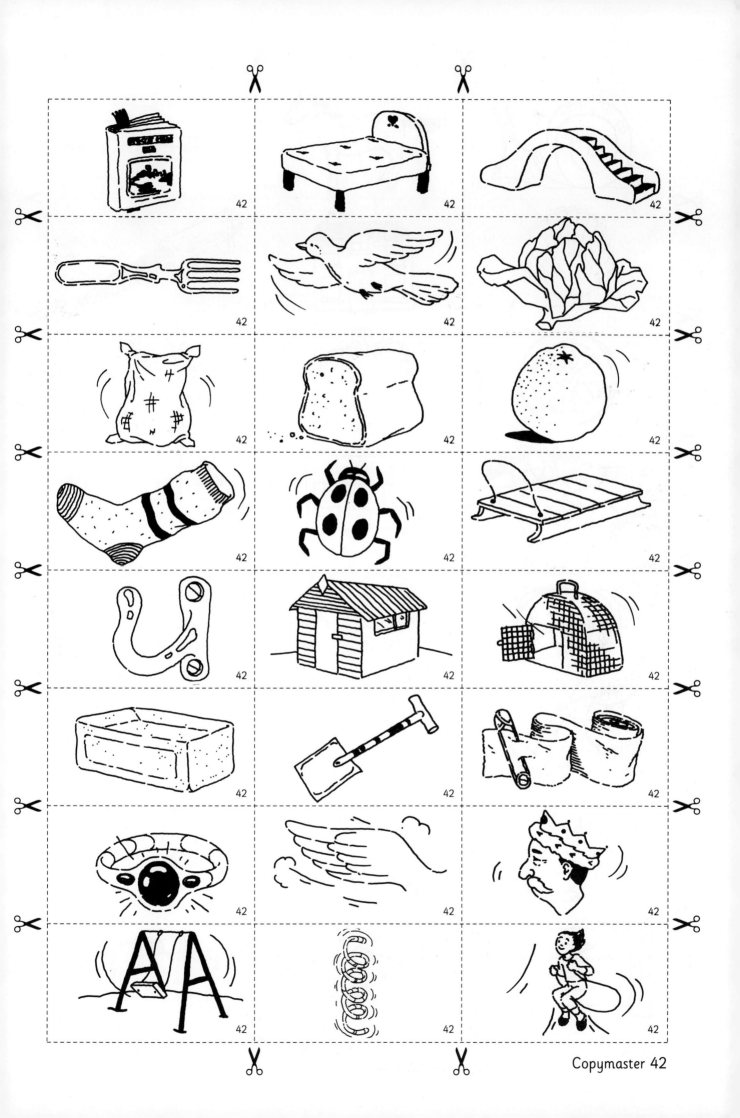

Copymaster 44

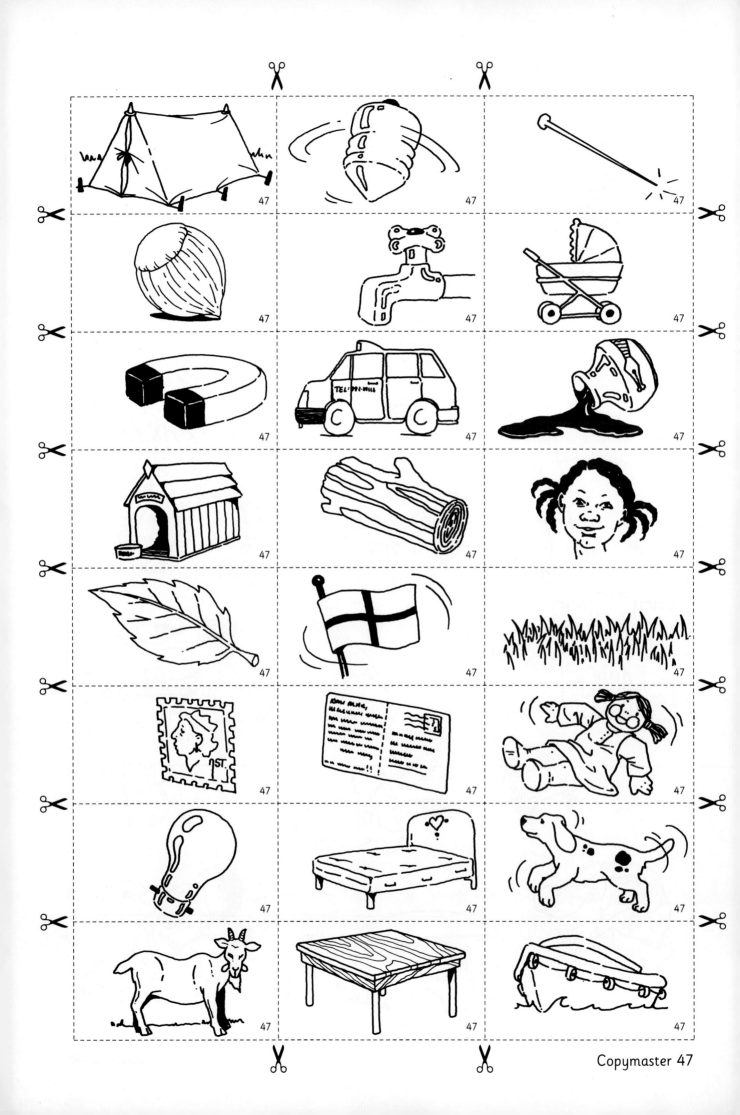

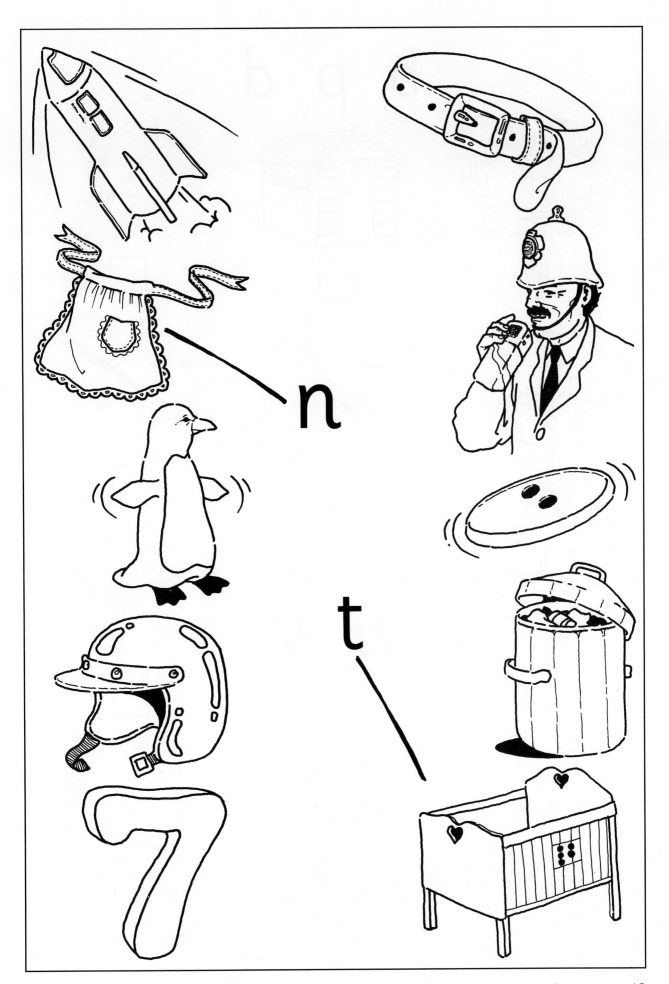

n

t

b p d

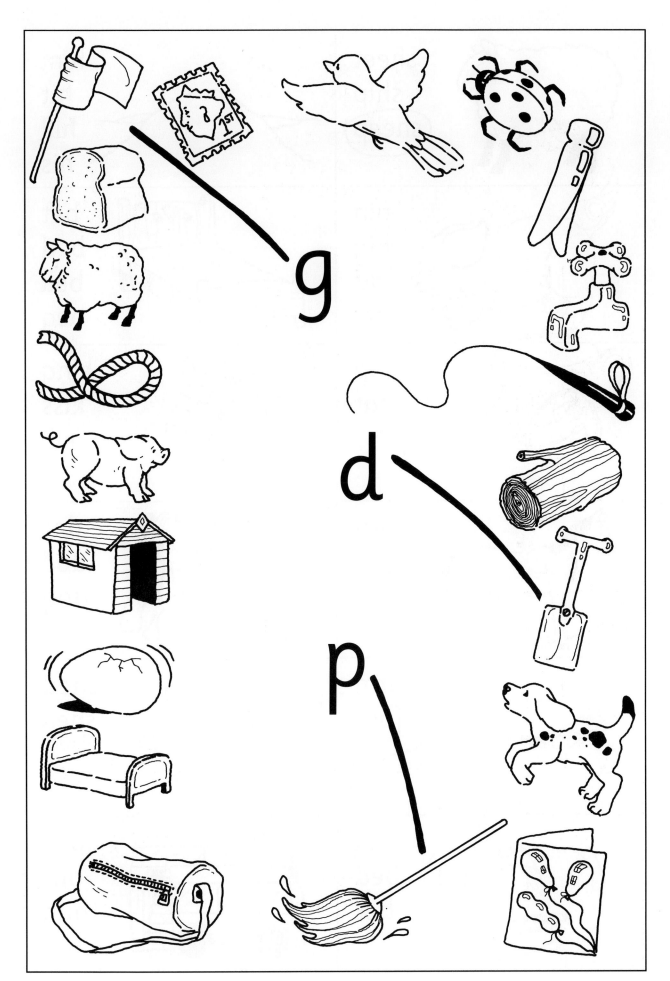

sheet ship (sheep)		him hit hill his	
pin pig pit pill		bet bed bell beg	
cap cat		king kiss kill	
horn horse		dot doll dog	
form fork		shed shell	
bell bed bet		bus but bun	

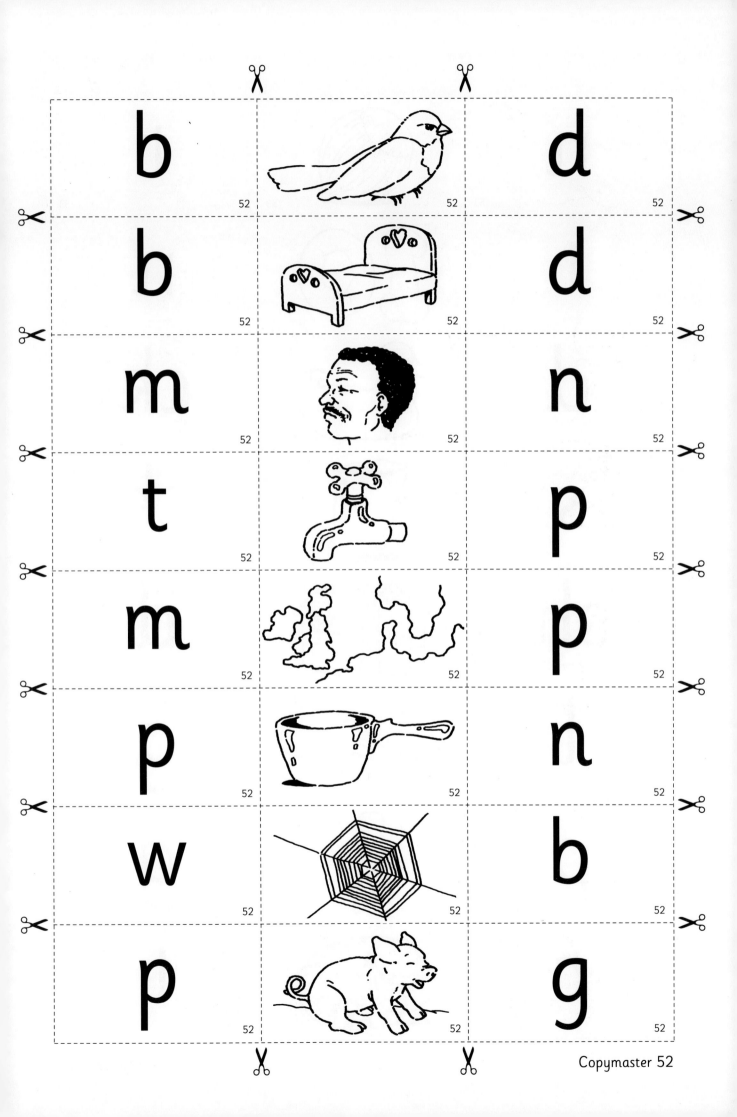

b   52   52   d   52

b   52   52   d   52

m   52   52   n   52

t   52   52   p   52

m   52   52   p   52

p   52   52   n   52

w   52   52   b   52

p   52   52   g   52

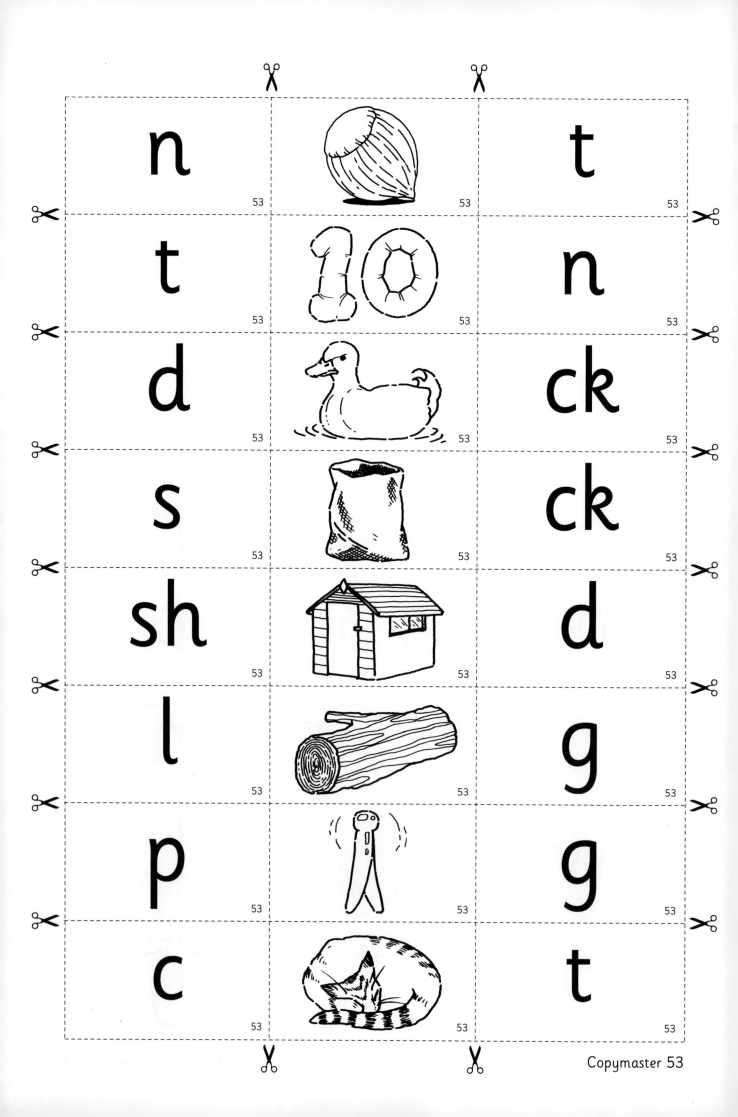

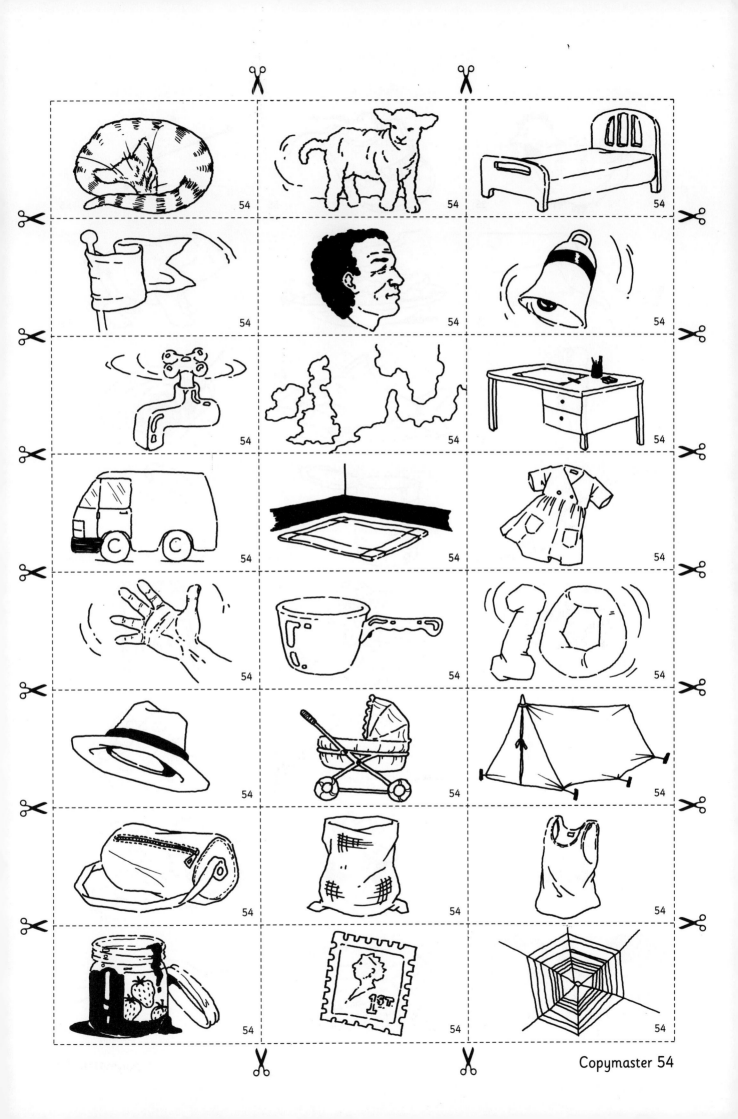

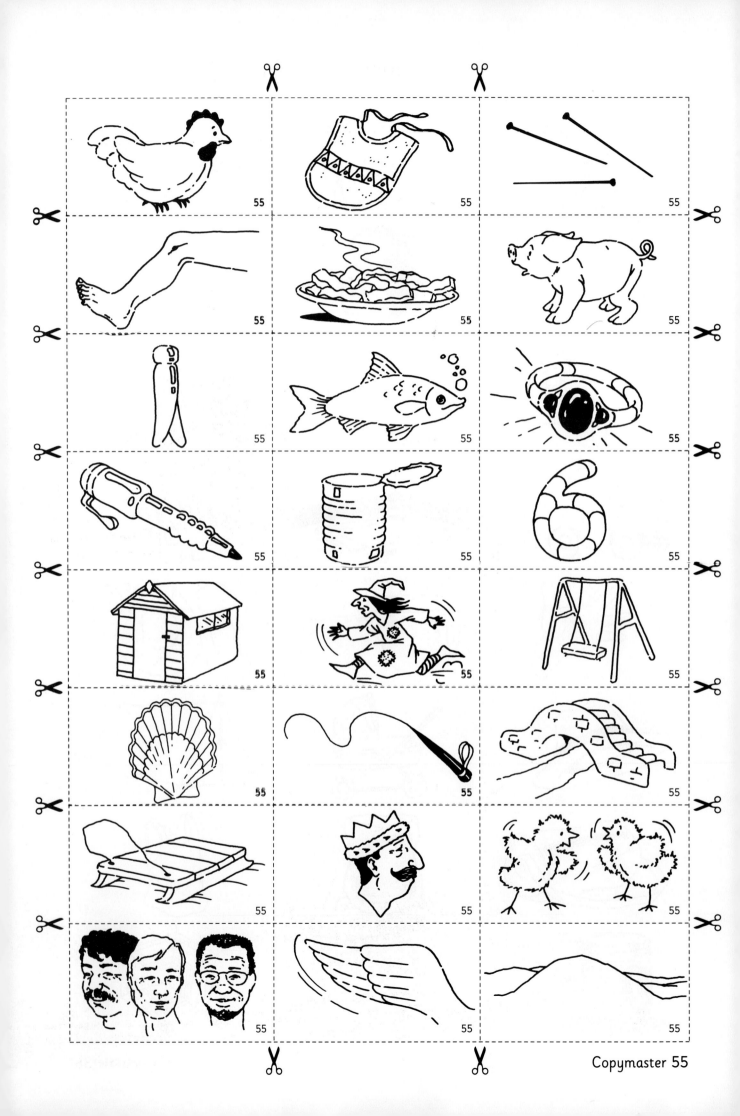

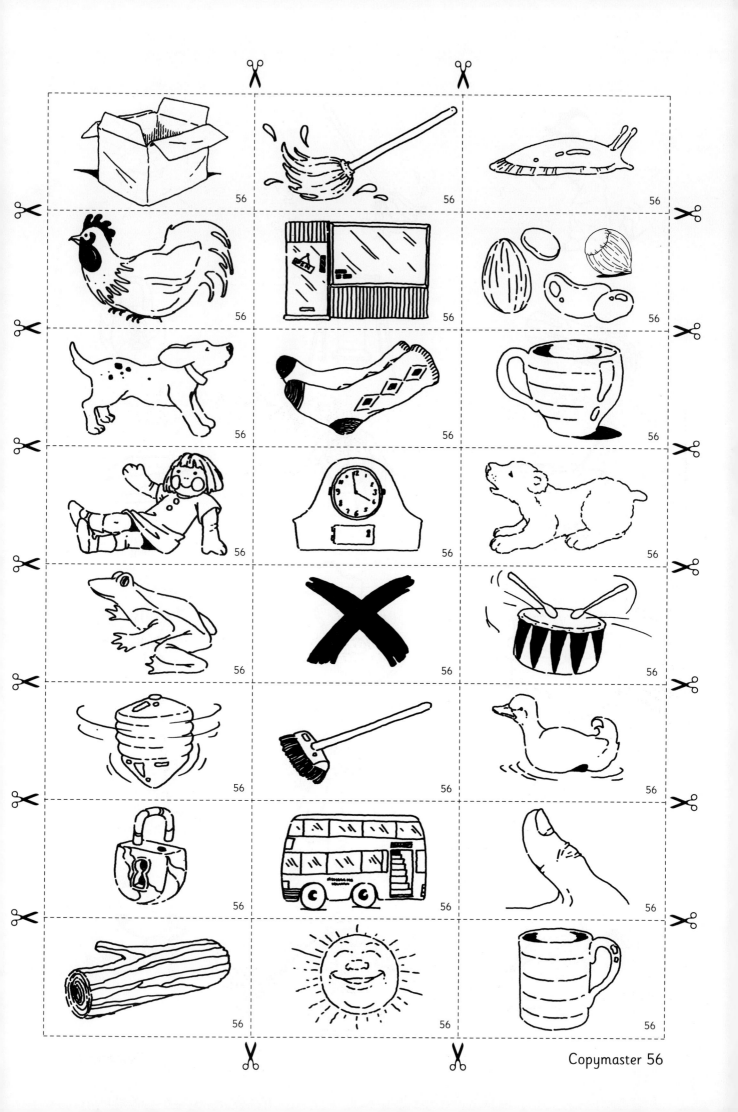

56
56
56
56
56
56
56
56
56
56
56
56
56
56
56
56
56
56
56
56
56
56
56
56

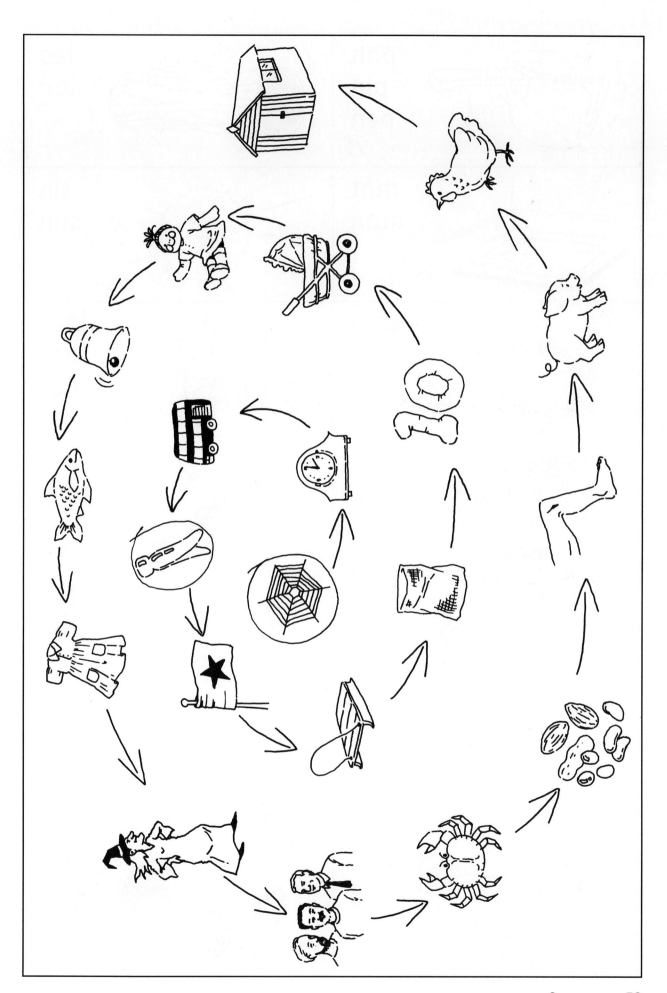

	(pan) pin pen		leg log
	mat man		sin sun
	ship shop		lock luck lick
	cap cup		watch witch
	bell bill ball bull		ten tin tan
	top tap tip		hot hat hut
	peg pig		sack sock sick

a e

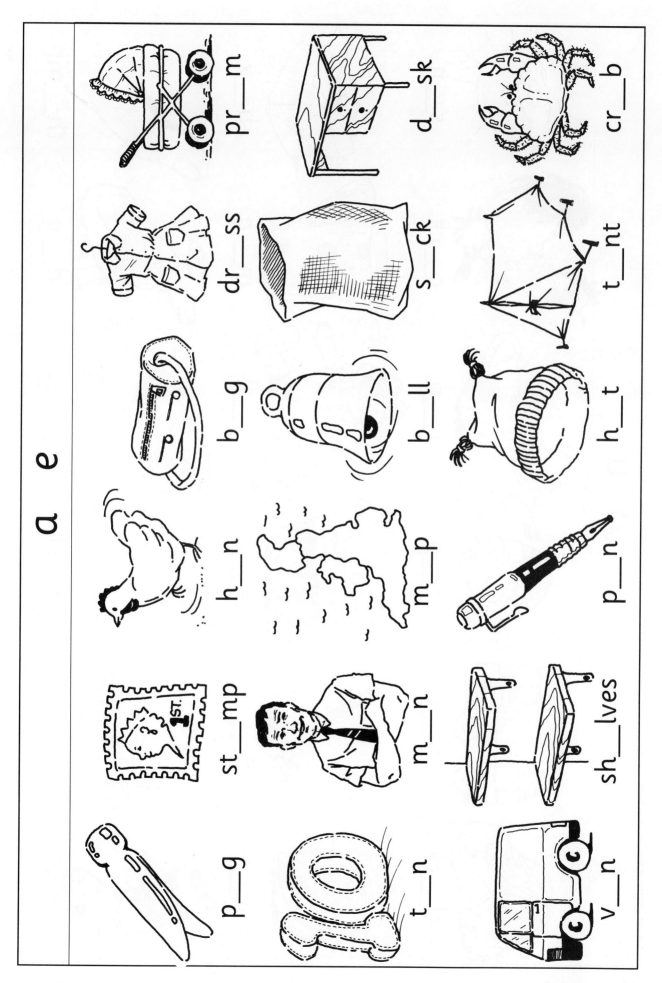

pr_m

d_sk

cr_b

dr_ss

s_ck

t_nt

b_g

b_ll

h_t

h_n

m_p

p_n

st_mp

m_n

sh_lves

p_g

t_n

v_n

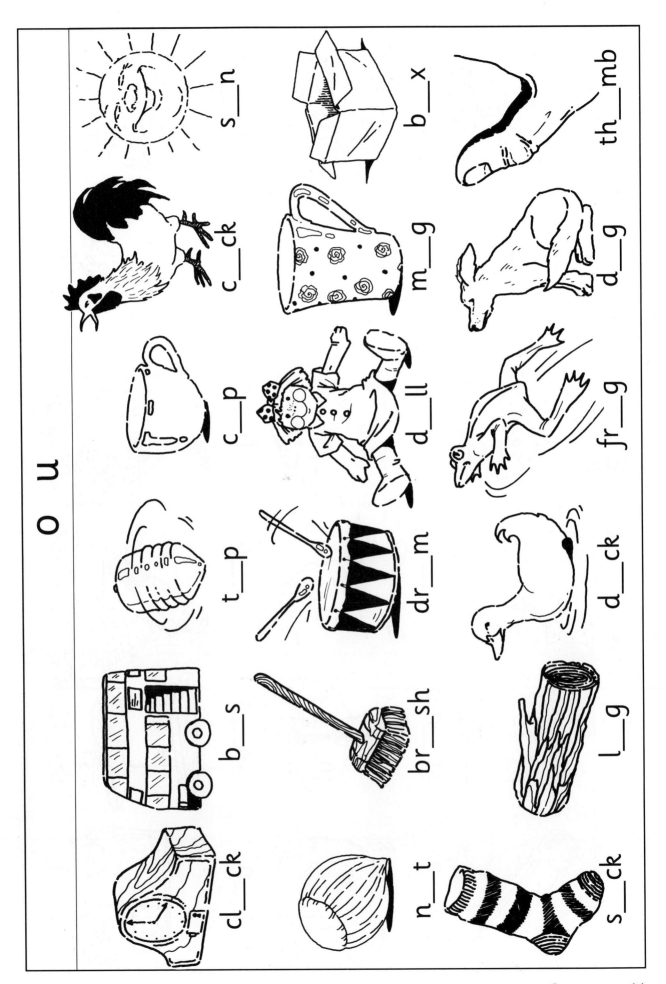

o u

s_n

b_x

th_mb

c_ck

m_g

d_g

c_p

d_ll

fr_g

t_p

dr_m

d_ck

b_s

br_sh

l_g

cl_ck

n_t

s_ck

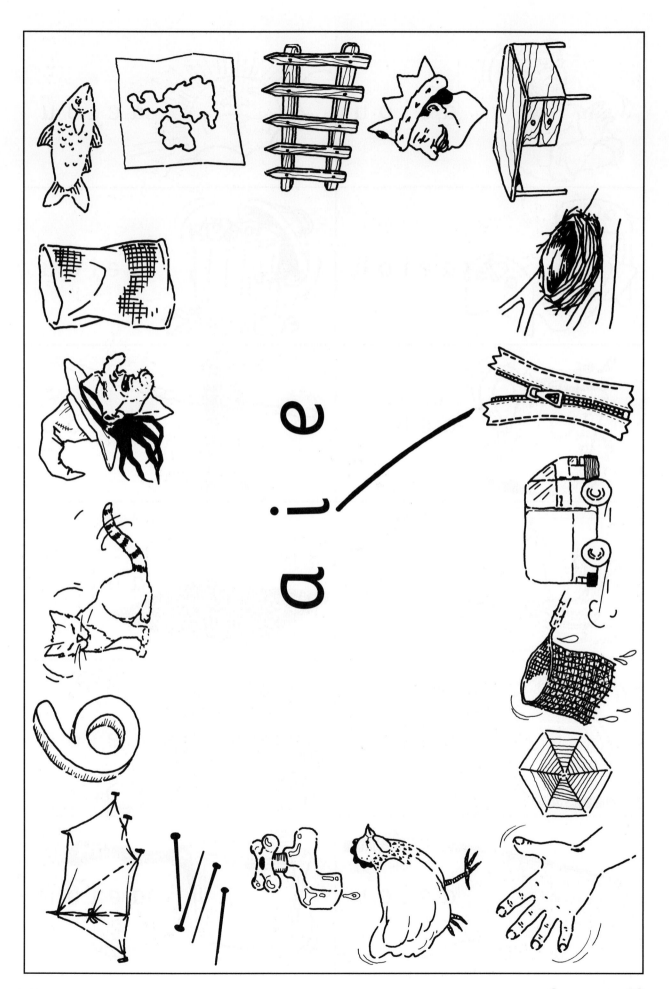

a i e

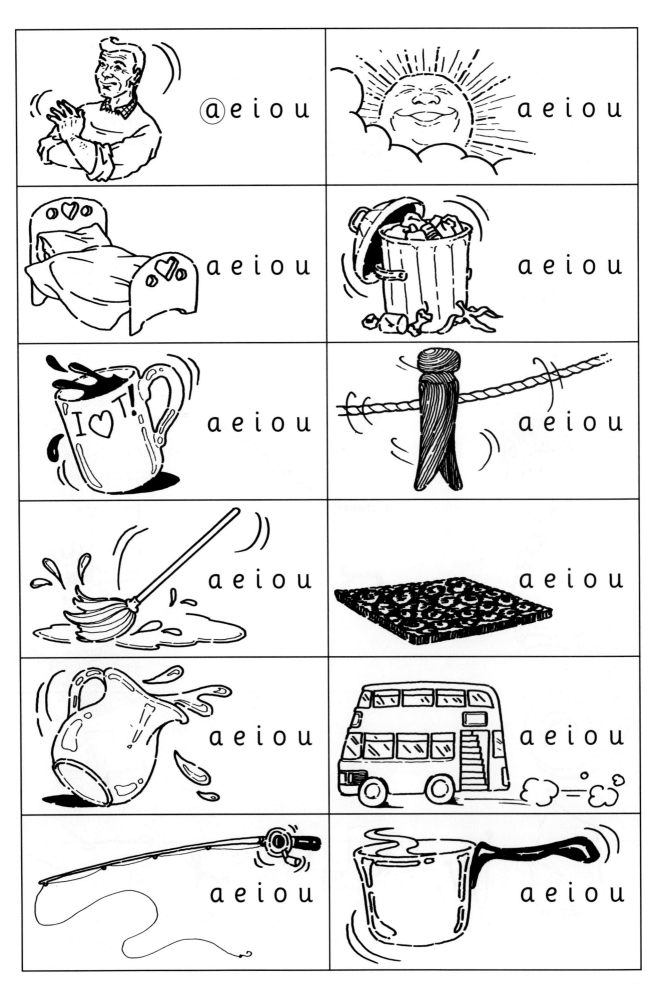

i e

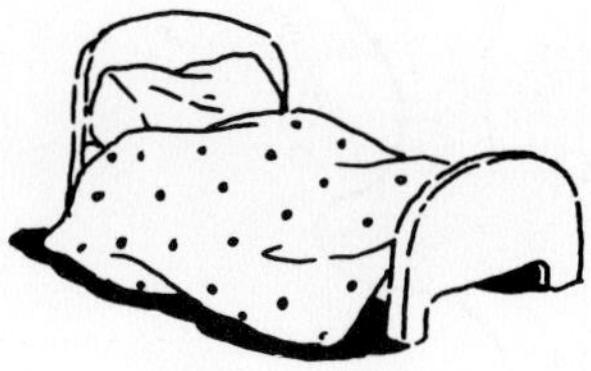

b__d 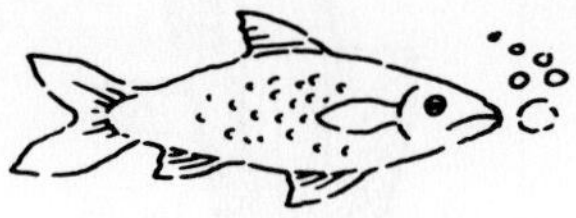   f__sh 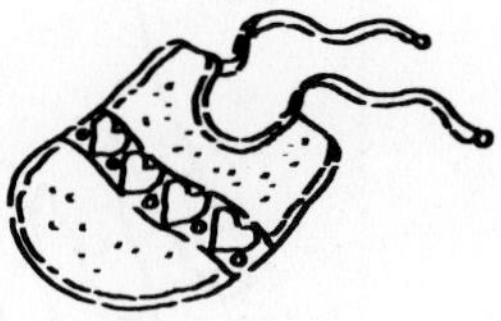   b__b

r__ng    b__ll    k__ng

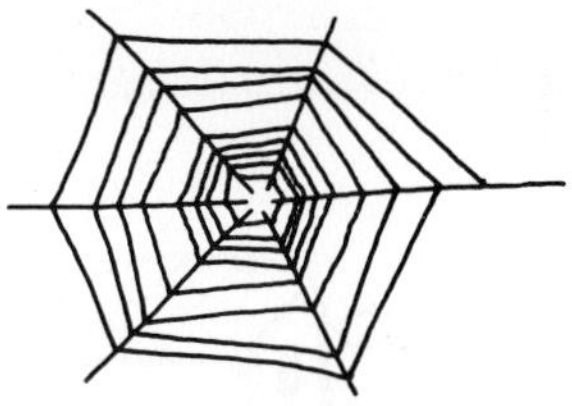

w__b 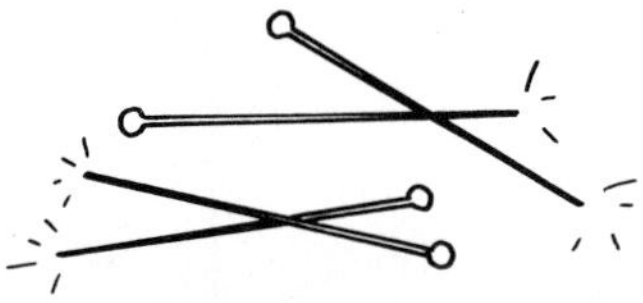   p__ns    t__n

p__g    v__st    s__x

br__dge    m__n    p__g

sh__ll    ch__cks    sh__d

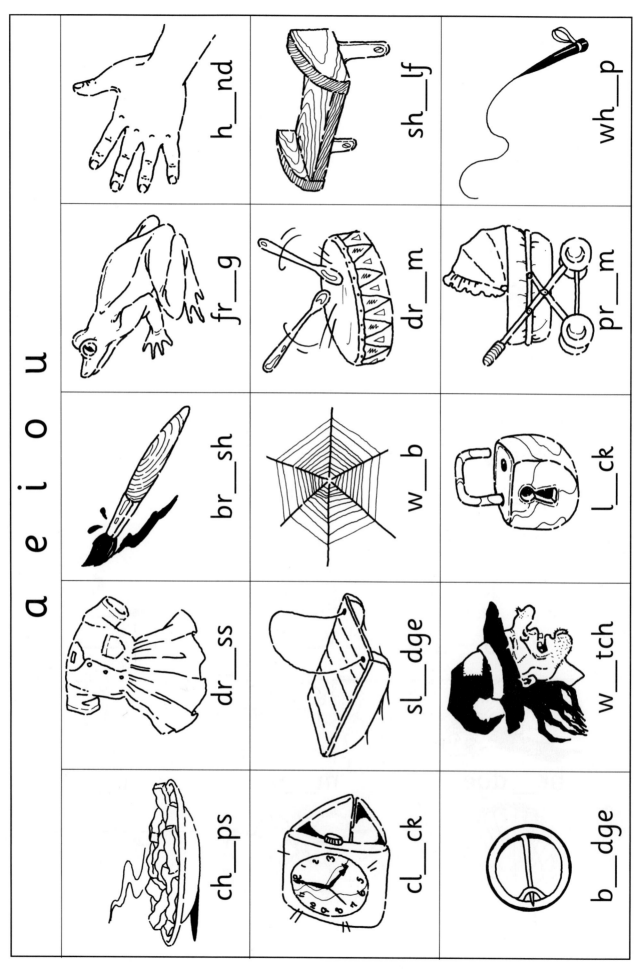

a e i o u

h_nd

sh_lf

wh_p

fr_g

dr_m

pr_m

br_sh

w_b

l_ck

dr_ss

sl_dge

w_tch

ch_ps

cl_ck

b_dge

Name

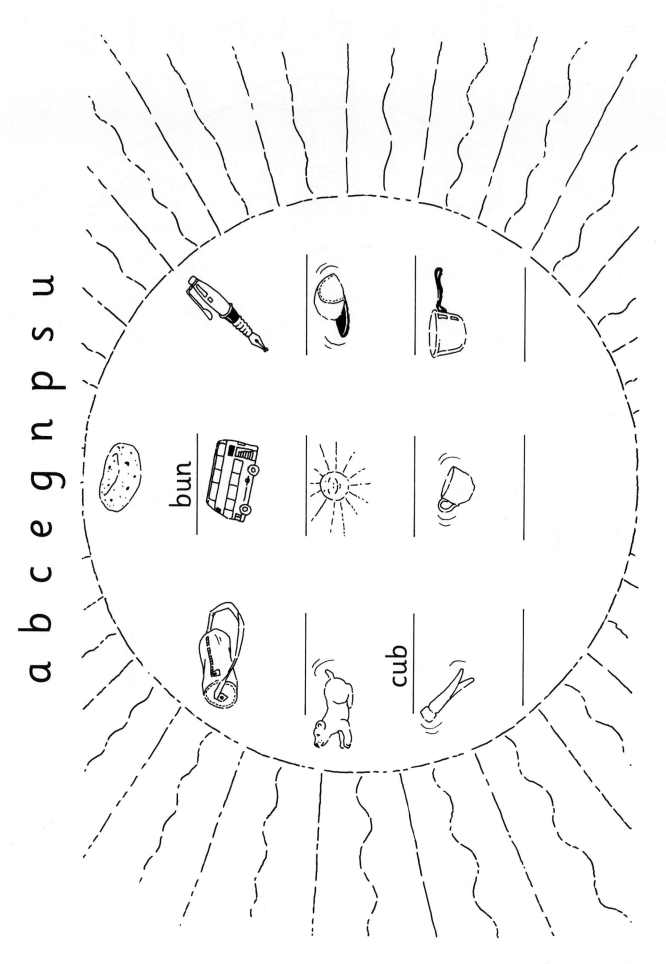

a b c e g n p s u

bun

cub

a i o u sh t m p f c

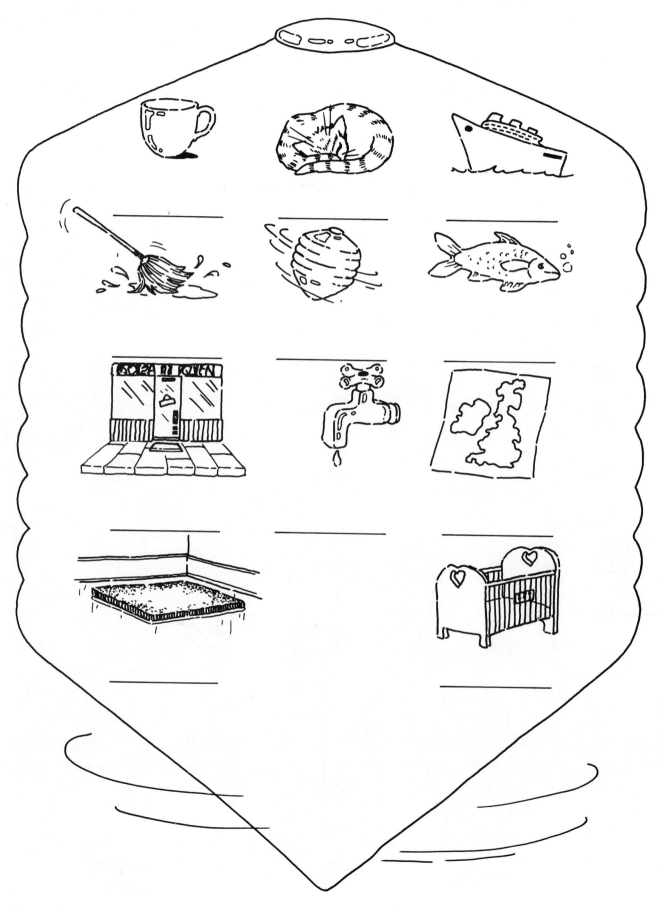

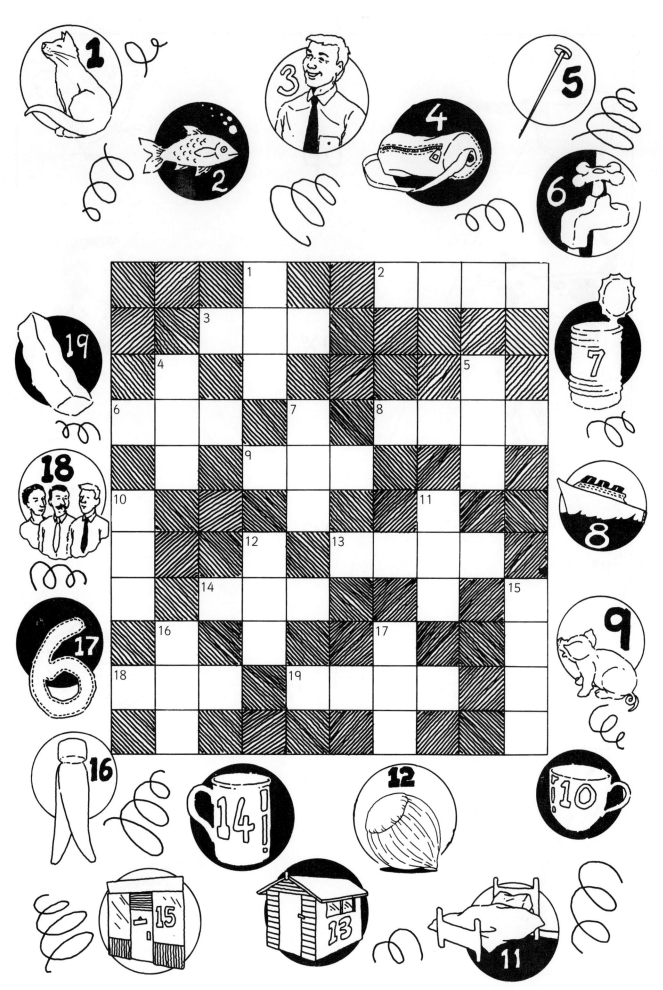

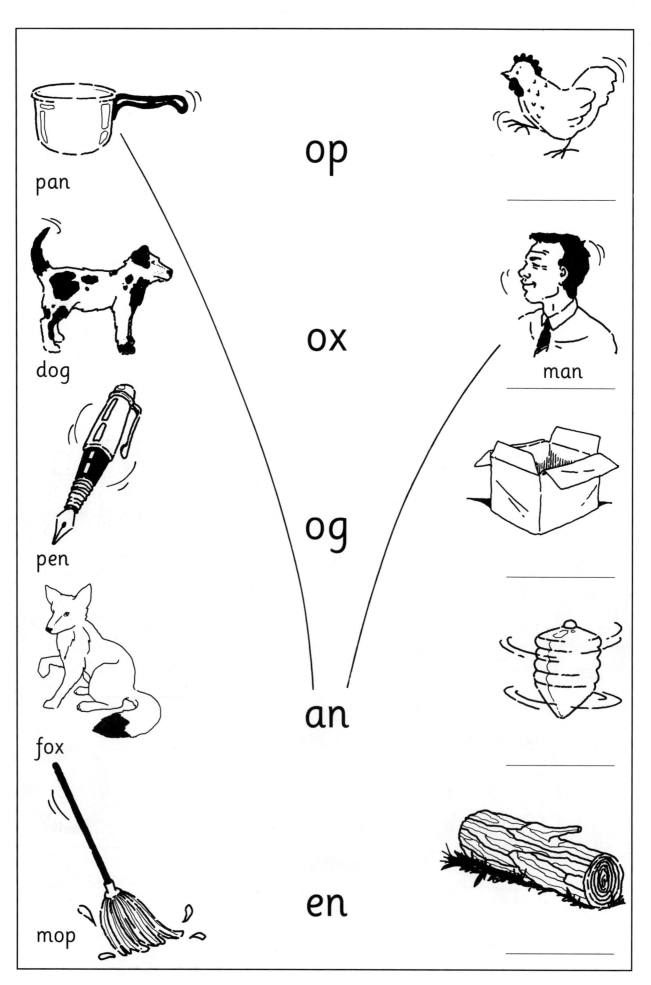

pan

dog

pen

fox

mop

op

ox

og

an

en

man

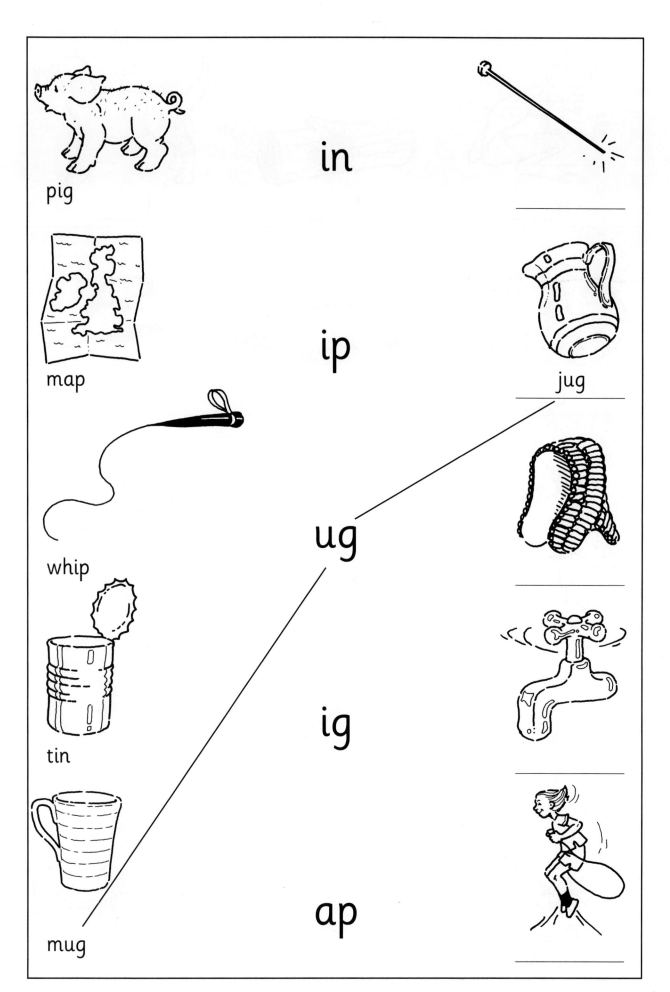

pig

map

whip

tin

mug

in

ip

ug

ig

ap

jug

fr___   l__   d___

c___   m___   h___

sh___   ch___   wh___

h___   p___   t___

m___   t___   sh___

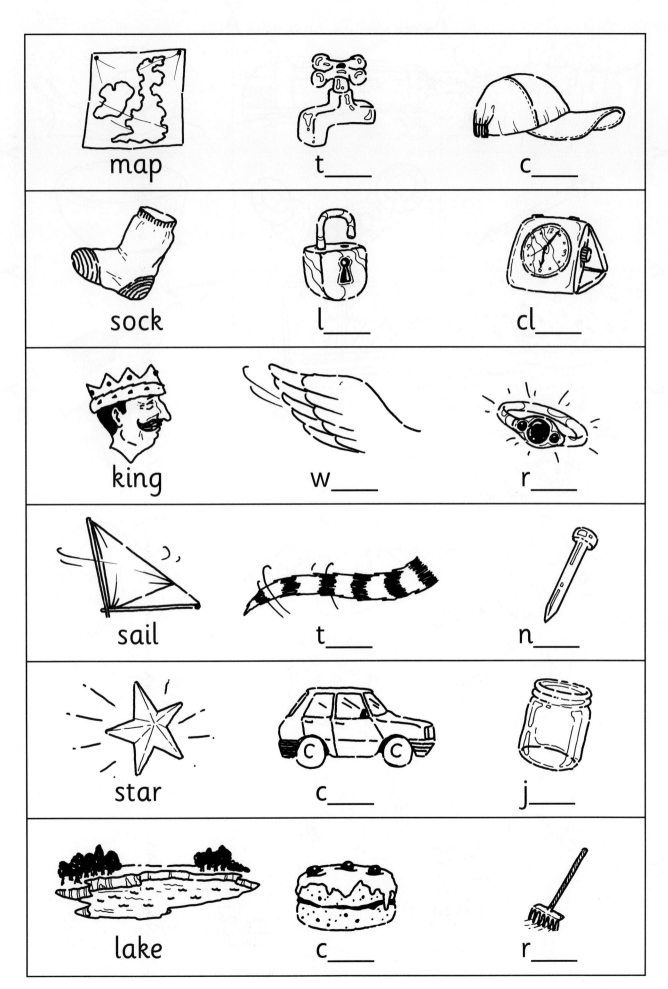

map

t___

c___

sock

l___

cl___

king

w___

r___

sail

t___

n___

star

c___

j___

lake

c___

r___

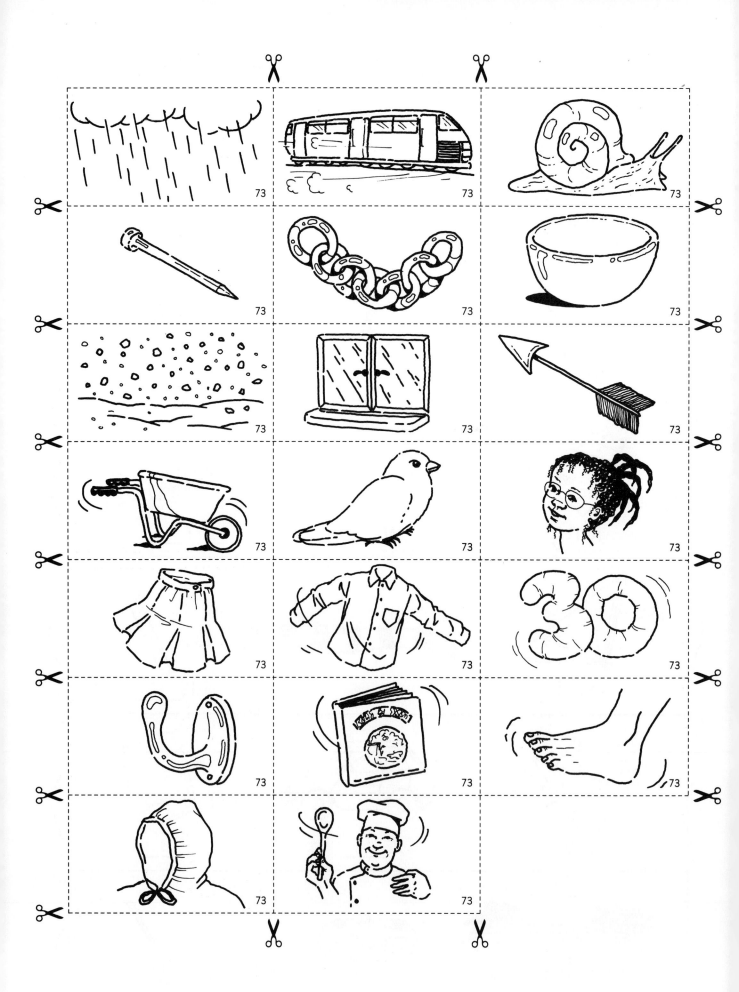

rain	bowl
train	snow
nail	window
snail	arrow
chain	barrow
74	74
bird	hook
girl	book
skirt	foot
shirt	hood
thirty	cook
74	74

Copymaster 74

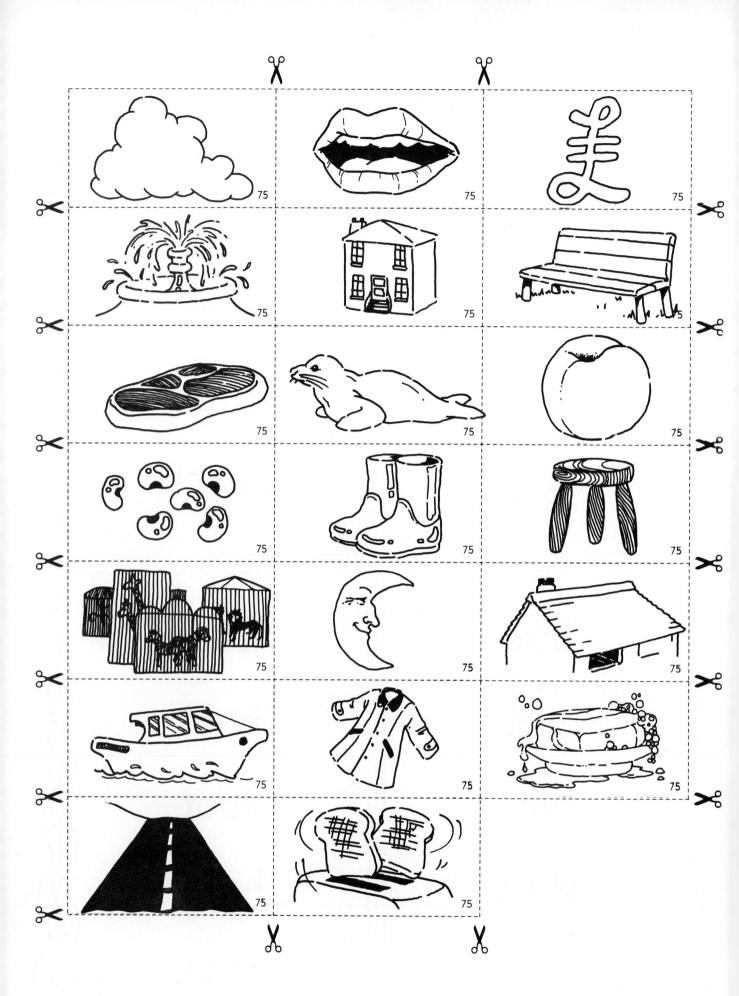

boots	boat
stool	coat
zoo	soap
moon	road
roof	toast

76

76

cloud	seat
mouth	meat
pound	seal
fountain	peach
house	beans

76

76

owl

clown

crown

down

cow

car

star

cart

shark

arm

78

78

fork

forty

horn

torch

corner

feet

sweets

sheep

wheel

queen

78

78

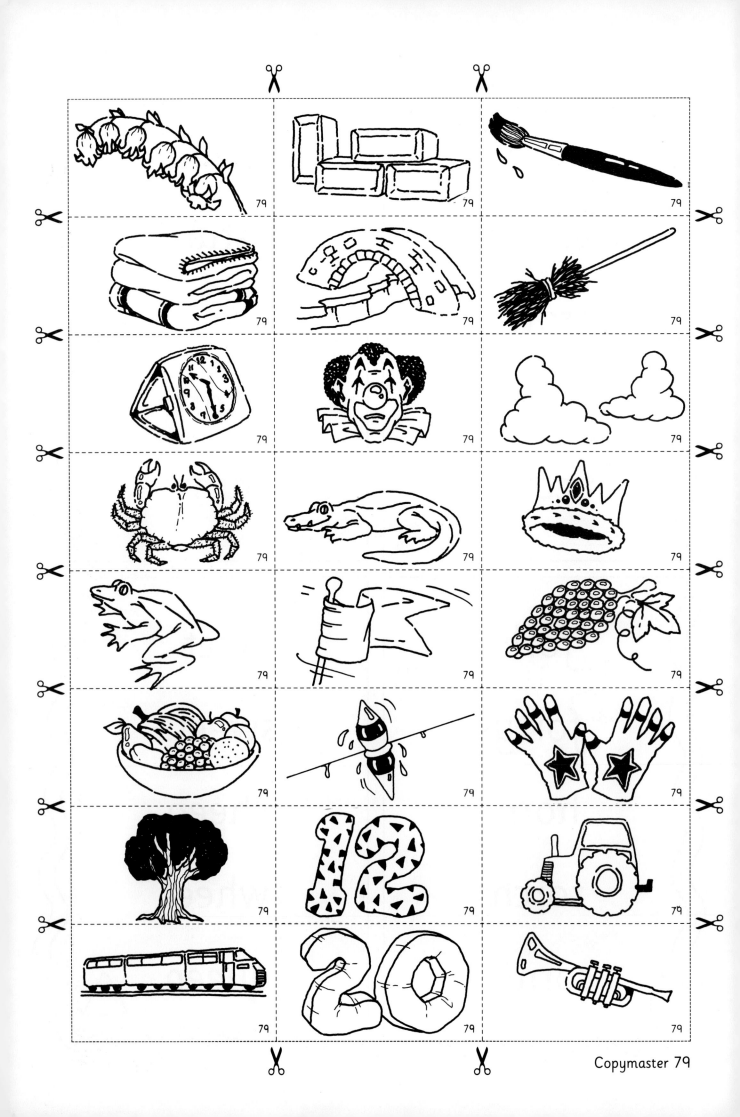

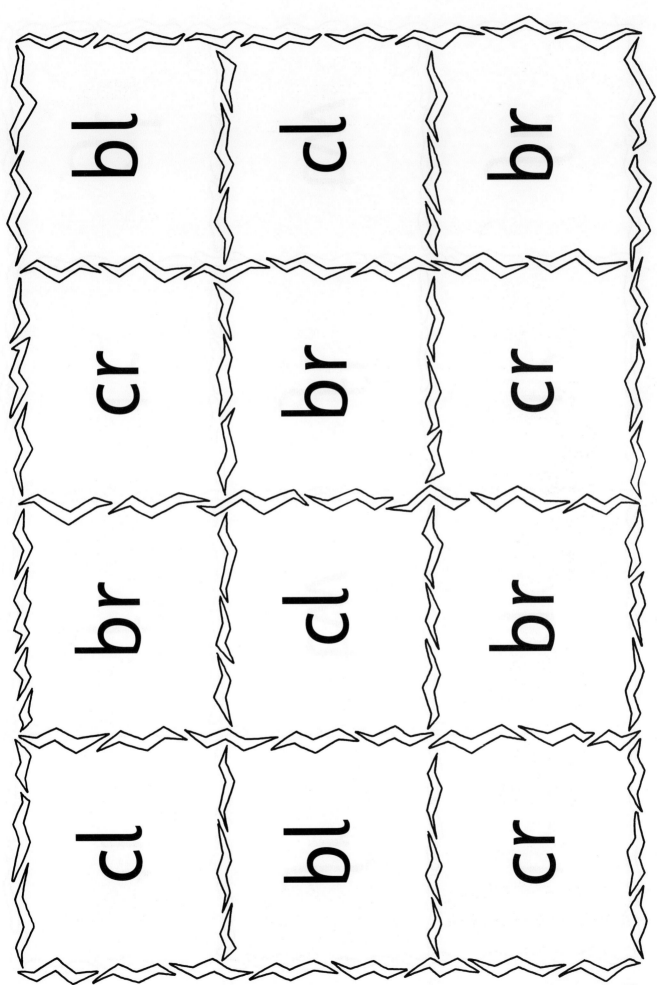

fr	tw	gl
tr	fl	tr
gr	tw	fl
tr	fr	tr

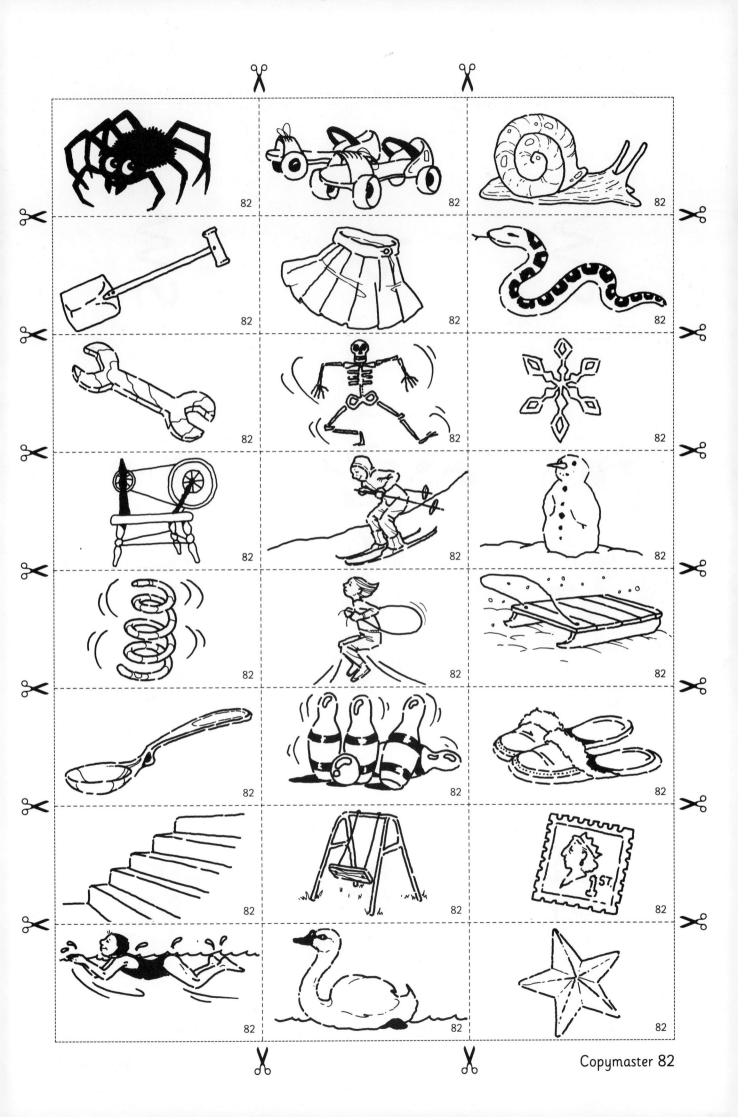

sw

sl

sw

sn

sp

st

sk

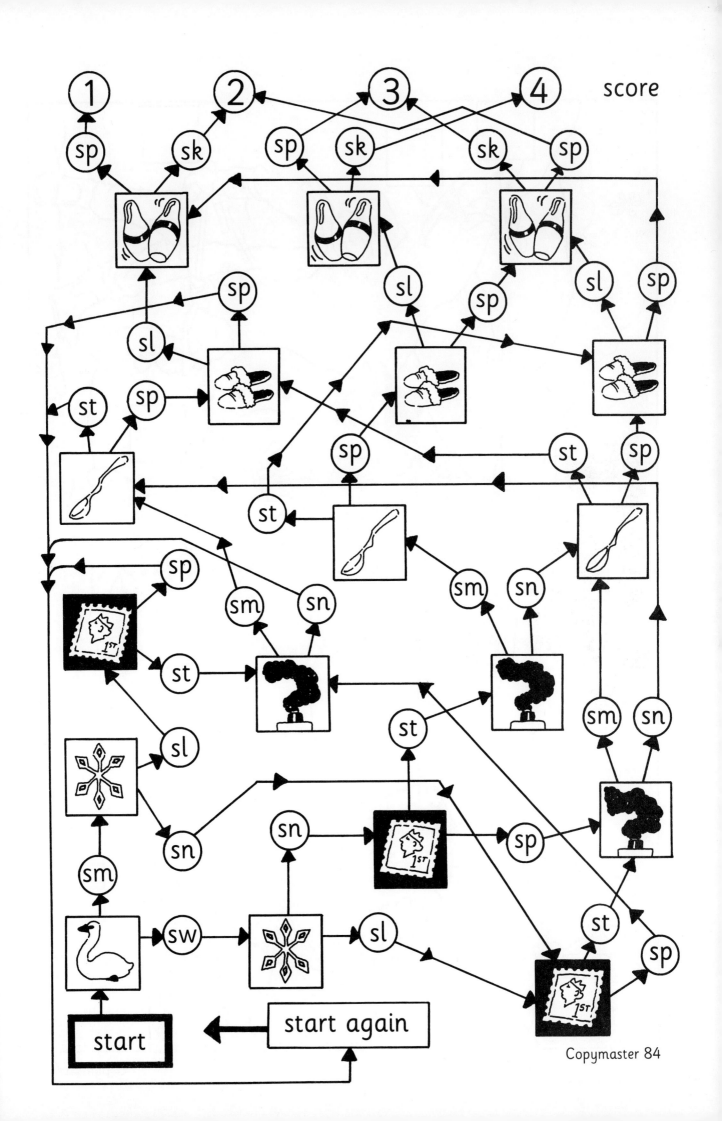

score

Copymaster 84

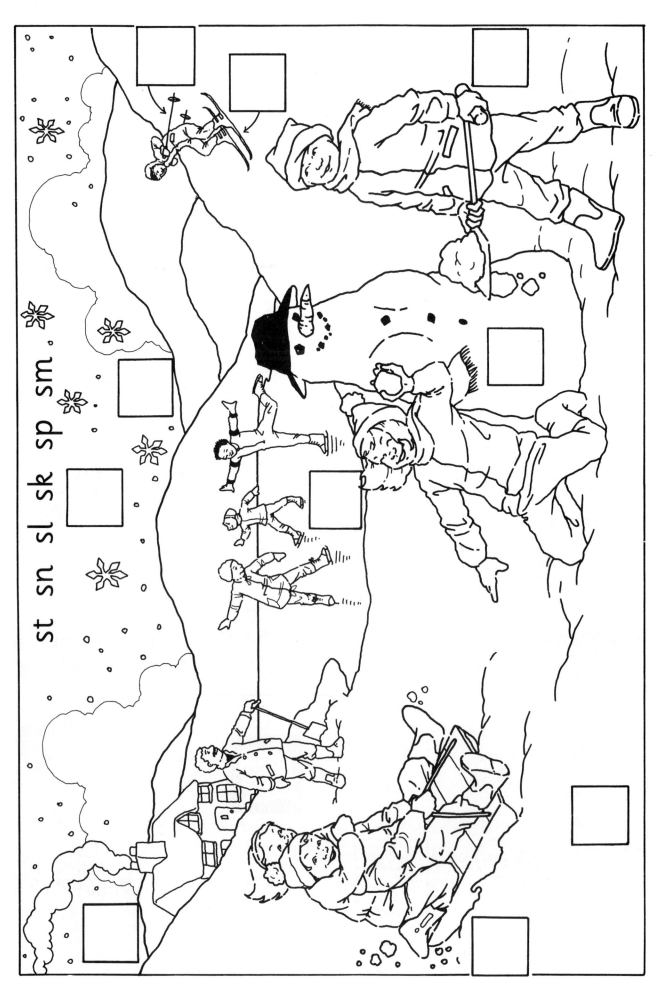

st sn sl sk sp sm

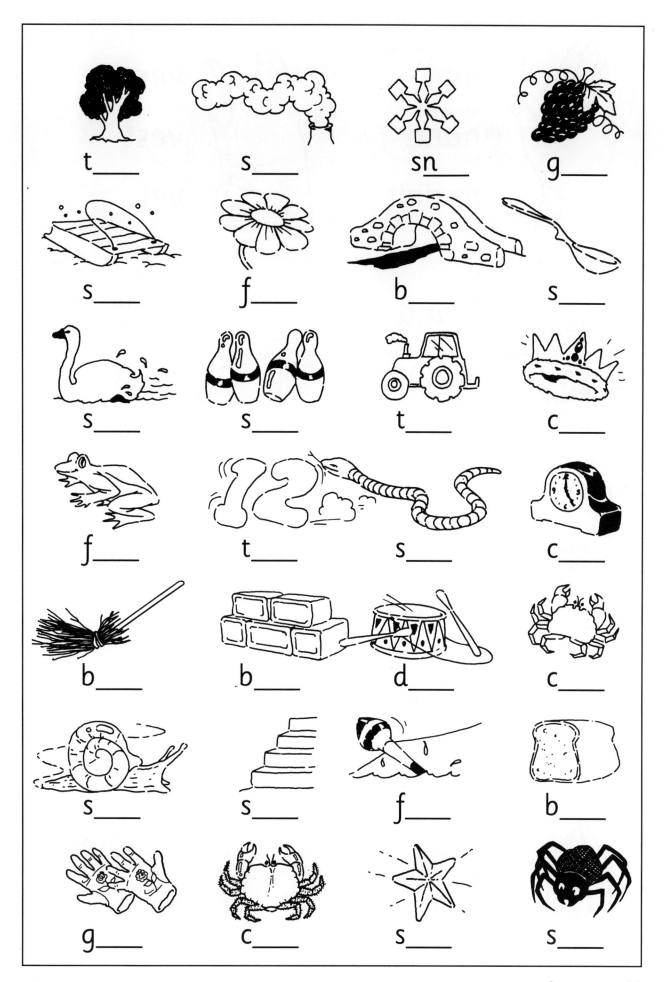

t____   s____   sn____   g____

s____   f____   b____   s____

s____   s____   t____   c____

f____   t____   s____   c____

b____   b____   d____   c____

s____   s____   f____   b____

g____   c____   s____   s____

Copymaster 86

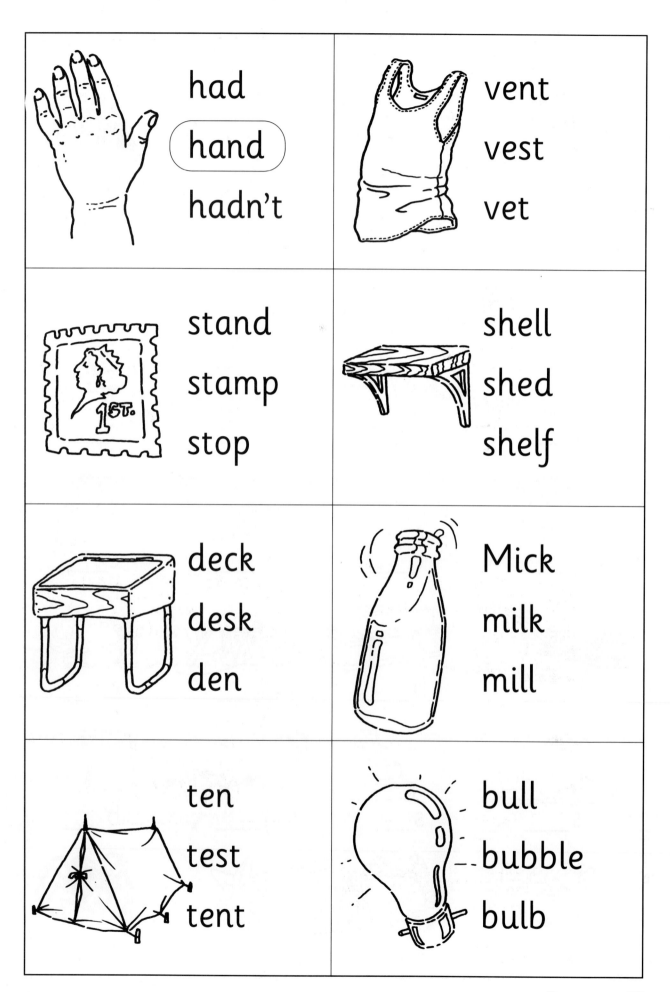

had
(hand)
hadn't

vent
vest
vet

stand
stamp
stop

shell
shed
shelf

deck
desk
den

Mick
milk
mill

ten
test
tent

bull
bubble
bulb

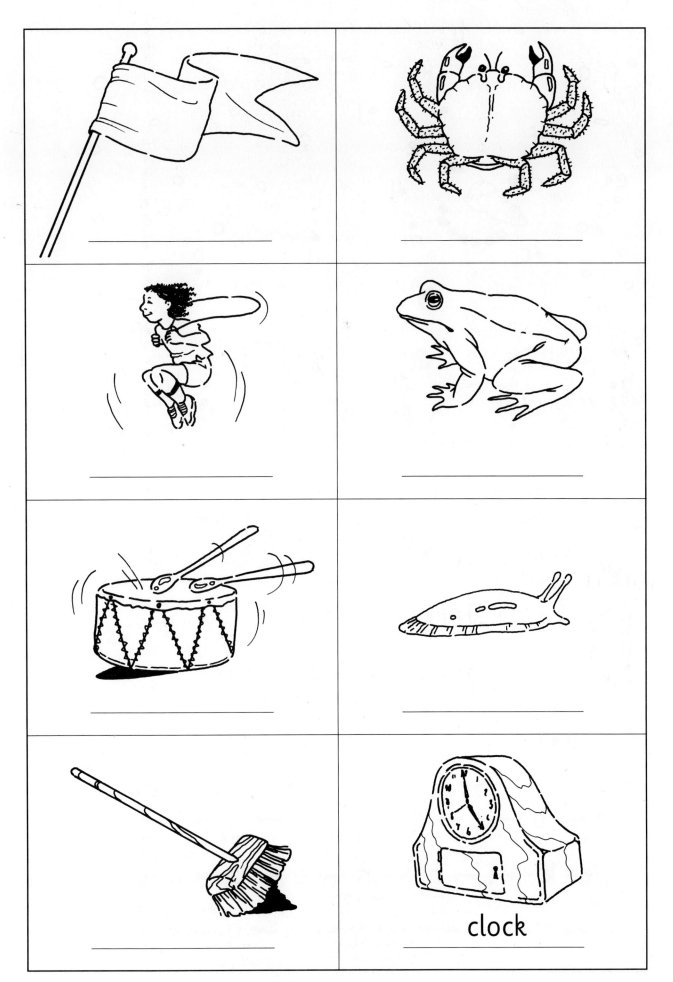

clock

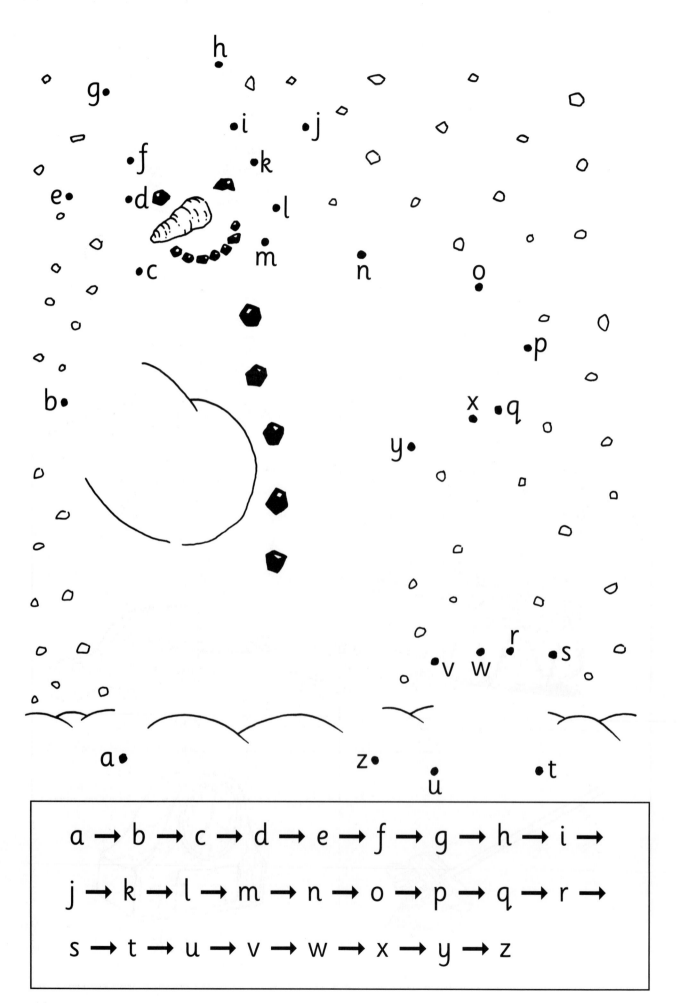

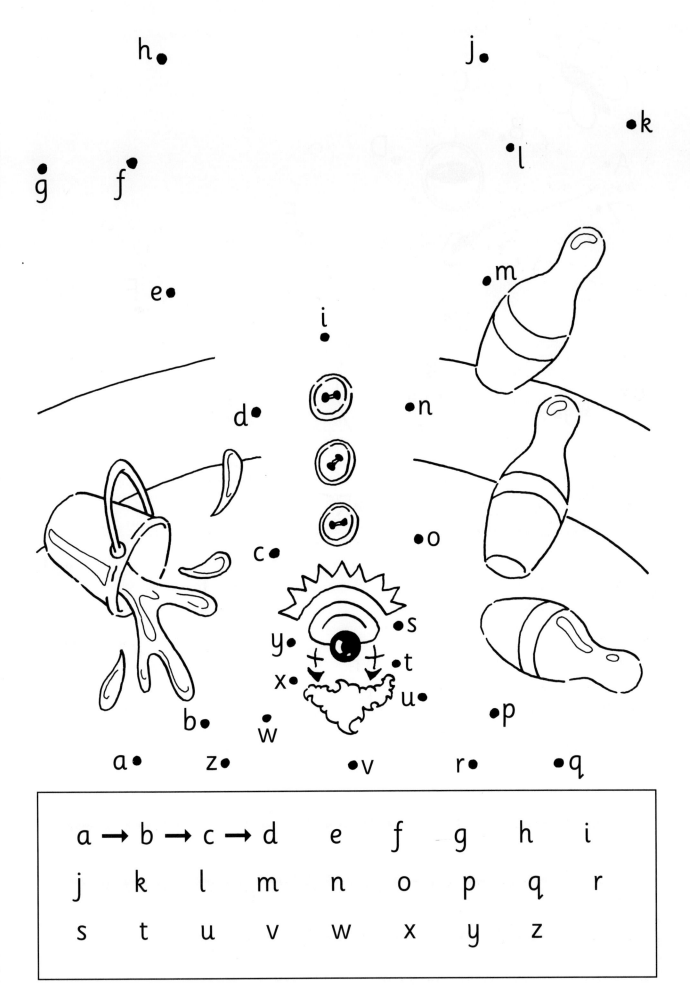

a → b → c → d   e   f   g   h   i

j   k   l   m   n   o   p   q   r

s   t   u   v   w   x   y   z

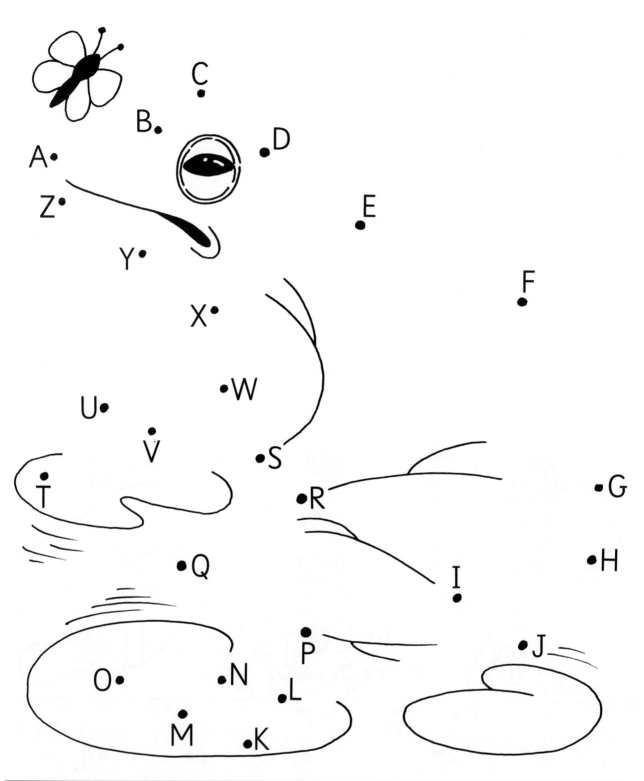

A → B → C → D → E → F → G → H → I →

J → K → L → M → N → O → P → Q → R →

S → T → U → V → W → X → Y → Z

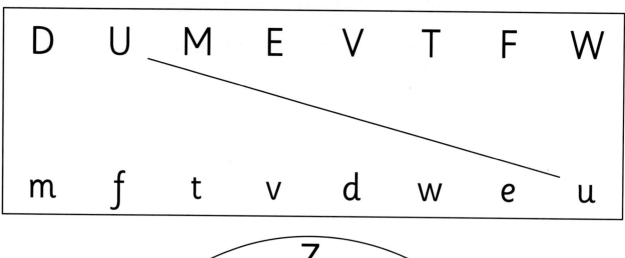

D U M E V T F W

m f t v d w e u

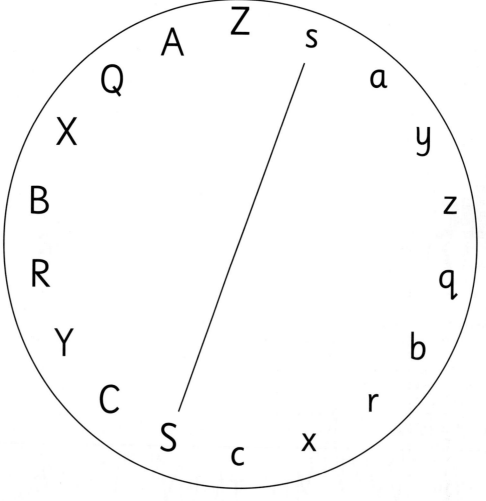

Q A Z s a

X y

B z

R q

Y b

C r

S x

c

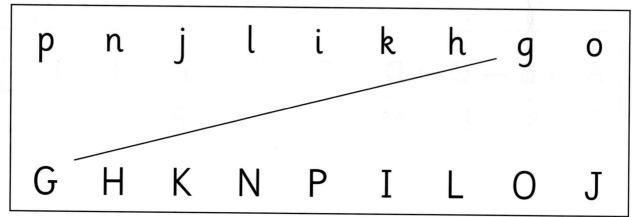

p n j l i k h g o

G H K N P I L O J

PART 2
LATER SPELLING

The title Later Spelling is deliberately vague. The first part of this book describes an approach which children are able, and mostly willing, to adopt in their spelling and which gives them a certain amount of independence in their writing. This approach requires children to write appropriate letters for the sounds which they can hear in words. They might, however, also learn to spell some words through familiarity with their visual forms, e.g. their own names and those of close friends and family, 'love from', etc.

The increasing use of this visual approach is what differentiates later from early spelling. Children who can hear middle vowel sounds in words have reached a point at which they can represent all the sounds in many common words such as 'said', 'was' and 'when'. Using the approach of matching letters to sounds, these words may be written 'sed', 'wos' and 'wen'. These are among the words most frequently used in the English language, and the children might repeat these forms of the spelling many times before recognising their errors. The motor patterns may then be difficult to unlearn. To prevent this, once children can represent the middle vowel sound in their spellings of words, they should be shown the conventional spellings for the most commonly used words. However, the decision to ask children to use a different approach for certain words should depend on the teacher's estimation of each child's attitude to writing. The teacher should help each child to balance the various elements of the writing process.

According to research, when we write we use certain words over and over again, so that about half of our writing tends to comprise approximately a hundred words, and these are common to all users of English. Frequency counts of these words made in Britain (Reid, D., Word for word. Wisbech: LDA, 1989) and the United States (Caroll J. B., Davies B. and Richman B., The word frequency book. New York: Houghton Mifflin, 1971) show considerable overlap, but disagree on certain words. I have amalgamated the two lists to produce the following 135 words:

a	for	my	their
about	from	name	them
after	get	new	then
again	go(ing)	next	there
all	good	night	these
an	got	no	they
and	had	not	this
another	has	now	three
are	have	of	time
as	he	off	to
at	her	old	too
away	here	on	took
back	him	once	tree
ball	his	one	two
be	home	or	up
because	house	our	us
bed	how	out	very
been	I	over	want
big	if	people	was
but	in	put	water
by	is	ran	way
call(ed)	it	said	we
came	last	saw	went
can	like	school	were
come	little	see	what
could	look(ed)	seen	when
dad	made	she	who
day	make	should	will
did	man	so	with
do	many	some	would
dog	may	take	yes
door	me	than	you
down	more	that	your
first	mum	the	

In order to find out which words children can and cannot spell, their work can be examined or they can be tested. The advantage of a test is that it is quick, and children can be grouped on the results of the test for teaching purposes.

The following pages contain assessments for seventy of these words. Suggestions for teaching all 134 and other related words appear on subsequent pages.

107

ASSESSMENT

There are six 'spelling tests' in this section to test children's knowledge of the following words.

about	day	is	our	they
after	do	last	out	this
all	down	like	over	three
and	for	little	play	too
are	from	made	put	two
away	go	make	said	us
back	has	me	saw	very
be	have	my	she	want
because	he	next	so	was
by	her	new	some	we
call	here	off	take	were
came	his	old	their	when
come	home	once	then	will
could	I	one	there	you

The assessments have been devised so that they are amusing and in no way threatening for children of six years of age. Children should not be alerted to the fact that they are being tested. However, it is necessary to ensure that they do not tell one another the answers or cannot see one another's answers to the tests. In order to avoid this:

• Only children who have attained the prerequisite level stated for the tests should be asked to do them. The prerequisite for the first three tests is that children can represent the middle vowel sound in their spellings of words. The lack of confidence of children who have not attained this level generally proves unsettling for them, and can disrupt the test for other children.
• Children could be spaced out at tables throughout the room. Children not doing the test could be working on some other quiet activity and sitting between those doing the test. Alternatively, if a small group is doing the test, they could all sit round one table, perhaps using cardboard boxes as 'polling booths'. Children find this fun and the teacher does not then need to lay great emphasis on 'not copying' when this may well conflict with the co-operative ethos within the class.

ASSESSMENTS 1–3

These assessments are intended for children who have shown an ability to represent three sounds in words, e.g. to write words such as 'big' and 'red' and approximations of words such as 'sed', 'woz', 'wen'. The assessments are in the form of stories about two children. The test words appear in positions in the sentences in which they are naturally stressed. Each test word is underlined, and each line containing a test word is preceded by a bullet point. These words are written in 'windows' in a house, a bus or in a balloon.

Procedure
Read the story to the children all the way through. Then read it again making sure that the underlined words are slightly stressed. At the end of the first line indicated with a bullet mark, stop and repeat the underlined word. Point to the top left window in the picture of the house or bus or to the top left balloon, and ask the children to write the word in the corresponding window/balloon on their pictures. Continue reading the story stopping at the end of each line indicated with a bullet point and pointing to the next window/balloon to be filled with a word.

Assessment 1 Martha's house
This test may be used to assess children's ability to spell the following common words:
'I', 'was', 'he', 'she', 'is', 'my', 'saw', 'when', 'there', 'and', 'they'.

Equipment
A photocopy of **Copymaster 94** and a pencil for each child and a large picture of 'Martha's house' drawn on a piece of sugar paper or white/black board visible to all the children. You also need the teacher's test sheet, page 109.

Assessment 2 On the bus to the zoo
This test may be used to assess children's ability to spell the following words:
'one', 'have', 'for', 'some', 'little', 'go', 'then', 'me', 'we', 'come', 'this', 'out'.

Equipment
One photocopy of **Copymaster 95** and a pencil for each child and a large picture of the bus drawn on a piece of sugar paper or white/black board visible to all the children. You also need the teacher's test sheet, page 110.

Assessment 3 The man with the balloons
This test may be used to assess children's ability to spell the following words:
'are', 'his', 'her', 'play', 'day', 'home', 'said', 'will', 'you', 'our', 'so', 'has'.

Equipment
One photocopy of **Copymaster 96** and a pencil for each child and a large picture of balloons drawn on a piece of sugar paper or white/black board visible to all the children. You also need the teacher's test sheet, page 111.

Assessment 1 Martha's house

Pani came round to Martha's house to see what she was going to do today. He found her upstairs, dusting. *(Show the children the top left hand window on Martha's house where she is dusting when Pani finds her.)*

Top row of windows
- 'My mum's going shopping but <u>I</u> have to stay here,' explained Martha.
(Repeat 'I' and tell the children to write it in the window.)
- 'I <u>was</u> going with her, but dad wants me to stay here to help him.'
(Repeat 'was', and tell the children to write it in the next window.)
- '<u>He</u> says he can't clean the house by himself.'
(Repeat 'he' and tell the children to write it in the next window.)
- 'But why doesn't your mum clean the house too? <u>She</u> is very good at it,' suggested Pani.
(Repeat 'she' and tell the children to write it in the next window.)

On the large picture of Martha's house show the children where to move to on the middle row of windows and continue repeating the underlined word in each line, as above.

- 'She certainly <u>is</u>,' replied Martha.
- Pani looked round the room. 'Isn't that <u>my</u> book about squirrels?' he asked.
- 'Yes,' agreed Martha. 'You left it here last week. I <u>saw</u> a squirrel yesterday.
- <u>When</u> I was going to the park, it was eating an acorn under a tree.

Bottom row of windows
- When I came back, it wasn't <u>there</u>.'
- 'I saw a squirrel <u>and</u> a rabbit once,' boasted Pani.
- '<u>They</u> were playing.'

Assessment 2 On the bus to the zoo

Top row of windows
- <u>One</u> day Martha and Pani were going by bus to the zoo with Pani's father.
- '<u>Have</u> you brought some apples?' asked Pani.
- 'What <u>for</u>?' said Martha.
- '<u>Some</u> of the keepers at the zoo let you give them to the elephants.

Second row of windows
- They like <u>little</u> ones best.'
- 'We will <u>go</u> to the penguins first,' decided Pani's father. 'They are fed at 11 o'clock.
- <u>Then</u> you can find the elephants.
- As for <u>me</u>, I shall read my paper for a little while.'

Third row of windows
- '<u>We</u> know where the elephants are, don't we Martha?' said Pani.
- '<u>Come</u> on, it's time to get off the bus.
- <u>This</u> way!'
- '<u>Out</u> you go,' said Pani's father.

Assessment 3 The man with the balloons

Pani's father took the children in through the gate of the zoo. There was a man selling great big balloons.
'We'll get one afterwards,' said Pani's father. 'We don't want to frighten the animals.'

Top row of balloons
- 'Are we going to be in time to watch the penguins being fed?' asked Martha.
- 'We will if we hurry,' said Pani's father.
- They ran so fast Martha nearly got left behind.

Next row of balloons
- 'You said we'd be in time,' panted Martha.
- 'You nearly weren't,' laughed Pani.
They watched as the penguins caught the fish in their beaks.
- 'Has that one got a fish?' asked Pani.

Next row of balloons
- 'I don't think so,' replied his father. 'It's not his turn yet.'
'How do you know it's a boy penguin?' asked Martha.
- 'Oh, all right then,' said Pani's father with a wink, 'her turn.'
- 'It's not even hungry. It just wants to play,' said Pani.

Bottom row of balloons
- 'She's like this every day,' said the keeper.
- 'She makes our job very difficult. We have to entice her to eat.
- If she doesn't hurry up I shall go home and leave her to her games.'
'Please may I try?' said Pani.
'Certainly,' said the keeper, handing Pani a wet fish.
Pani gently held out his hand. The penguin looked at him and then swam towards the edge of the water. She scrambled up the bank, waddled towards Pani and took the fish in her beak.
'Well done,' whispered the keeper. 'Try another one.'

ASSESSMENTS 4–6

The following three assessments are designed to test children's knowledge of thirty more of the words they are likely to need in their writing. They are intended for slightly older children, and include a sale poster and two stories about a family of rabbits. Unlike the first three assessments, the words in the stories in Assessments 4, 5 and 6 are not in stressed positions in the sentences.

Assessment 4
This test may be used to assess the children's ability to spell the following words:
'here', 'next', 'from', 'one', 'two', 'three', 'last', 'down', 'off', 'all', 'made', 'new', 'take', 'very', 'over' and 'too'.

Equipment
One photocopy of **Copymaster 97** per child and an enlarged version of this poster for display at the front of the class.

Procedure
Introduce the poster, which is advertising a sale in a shop. Explain that some of the words are missing and ask the children to insert them. Tell them which words to put where by pointing to the poster at the front of the class. The words to be spelled are on the completed poster below in small italics.
(Note: two spellings of the word two/too are presented here.)

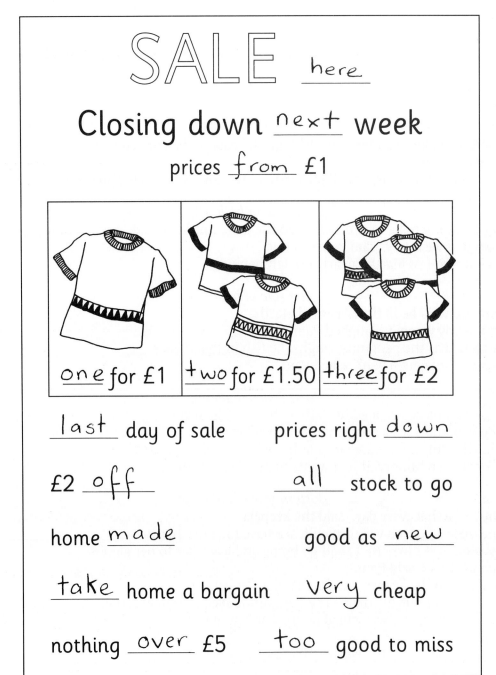

Assessment 5

This test may be used to assess the children's ability to spell the following words:
'after', 'away', 'because', 'call', 'came', 'could', 'do', 'old', 'once' and 'their'.

Equipment

Either photocopy **Copymaster 98** or give the children lined paper making sure that they understand that they are to write a new word on each line. Cut lined paper vertically so that each child has a narrow strip. This saves paper and will prevent the spellings becoming mixed up, thereby making marking easier.

Procedure

You may wish to read the whole story through to the children first. Or you may prefer the suspense of the story line to motivate the children to complete the assessment.

Read the story, stopping at the end of each of the lines preceded by a bullet point and repeat the word to be spelled.

- Once there lived a large brown rabbit in the side of a hill. *(repeat 'once')*
- He was very old. *(repeat 'old')*
- He could no longer see very well. *(continue repeating underlined word, as before)*
- His children, grandchildren, great grandchildren, nieces, nephews, great nieces and great nephews came to visit him.
- They told him stories of their adventures.
- After they had finished, he enthralled them with tales of his boyhood. He told them about the day he got shut in Mrs Scroggins' shed.
- He had crept in there because he was frightened. He was being chased by her dog.
- Mrs Scroggins had come to call him in for his supper.
- She had shut the door of the shed and gone away.
- He had not known what to do.

Assessment 6

This test may be used to assess the children's ability to spell the following words:
'about', 'back', 'be', 'by', 'like', 'make', 'put', 'us', 'want', and 'were'.

Equipment

As for Assessment 5 but using **Copymaster 99**.

Procedure

As for Assessment 5.

The old rabbit had found himself shut in Mrs Scroggins' shed.
- 'Tell us what happened next,' said all the younger rabbits.
- 'Well, I didn't like it much,' said the old rabbit.
- 'There were lots of strange smells.
- I started to look for a means of escape. The back of the shed was rotten.
- I decided to make a hole in the rotten wood.
- I had just about gnawed a hole big enough to squeeze through when I heard a squeaking noise.
- So I put my eye to the hole.
- Right by the house I could see Mrs Scroggins' cat playing around with a mouse.
- I could see it would not be long before the cat ate the mouse.
- I did not want that to happen; nor did the mouse.
I pushed through the hole. The rotten wood gave way. I hopped up to a metal bucket and gave it one enormous kick. It fell over with a very loud clatter. The cat looked round and saw me. He hesitated for a moment and then, as I had hoped, started to leap towards me. But I was faster than him and got clean away into the wood. Meanwhile the mouse had also disappeared.'

From the preceding assessments, you can compile a list of words now known by each child. Suggestions for teaching these words can be found on pages 115–118.

Further tests may be compiled from the remaining words from the list on page 107. The next 214 most frequently used words are as follows:

above	fair	moon	think
across	far	morning	those
against	father	mother	thought
air	feet	much	through
almost	fell	mummy	times
along	find	must	today
also	fish	near	together
always	five	need	told
am	following	never	top
animals	food	nice	trees
any	football	number	tries
around	found	often	try
asked	four	only	turned
baby	friends	opened	under
balloon	garden	other	until
bedroom	gave	outside	upon
before	girl	own	used
began	give	paper	walk(ed)
being	goes	park	(ing)
below	gone	part(s)	watch
best	great	place	well
better	hair	read	where
between	hand	red	while
bird	happy	right	white
birthday	hard	road	whole
bit	head	room	why
black	hear	round	wind
blue	heard	run	window
boat	help	sad	without
both	high	same	woke
boy	hole	say	wood
brother	I'm	sea	word
brought	important	second	work
brown	inside	shop	world
can't	its	show	write
car	it's	side	year
care	jumped	since	young
cat	just	sister	
change	keep	sky	
children	kind	sleep	
clothes	king	small	
cold	knew	snow	
coming	know	snowman	
cup	lady	something	
daddy	leave	sometimes	
dark	left	soon	
didn't	let	sound	
different	life	started	
dinner	light	still	
does	line	stopped	
don't	live(d)	story	
during	long	such	
earth	lost	suddenly	
eat	lot(s)	sun	
end	means	sure	
even	men	swimming	
ever	might	tea	
every	miles	tell	
eyes	money	thing(s)	

114

TEACHING LATER SPELLING

The suggestions in this section are based on the assumption that children can spell correctly regular monosyllabic words such as 'run' and 'ship', by matching the sounds they hear in the words to letters (see Part 1 Beginning to spell). They may also be writing 'said' as 'sed' and 'was' as 'wos'. It is not expected that they can hear such consonants as the 'r' in 'pram' or the 'n' in 'went', or know the possible sounds of the vowel digraphs 'ee', 'oa', etc. Work on early spelling to develop their ability to hear sounds in words and to learn and to recognise letters should continue alongside the strategies suggested in this section.

Later spelling requires the adoption of new strategies for learning to spell words and the application of these strategies to a specific body of words. The new strategies include looking for words within words, for words with common letter patterns or 'strings' for words which are linked by a consistently spelled stem and meaning and, if none of these are appropriate, for other mnemonics to enable particular words to be remembered. The specific body of words would include the hundred or so most frequently used words and a growing number of words relating to personal experience and subject matter covered in the classroom. Organising the body of words so that the children can begin to make connections between words in order to make learning easier is where the teaching starts.

LETTER-STRINGS
C100 –106

Encourage children to group words according to a common letter-string. Regular, phonemically constructed words such as 'an', 'on' and 'at' and irregular words such as 'one' and 'the' are also letter-strings common to other words, e.g. 'then', 'them', 'there' and 'their'. Children can be taught to look for words within words or the same group or string of adjacent letters in a number of different words. This can be achieved as a class while reading a 'big book' or as an individual or a group activity. Children could also bring words found at home and a pin board could be allocated for words which contain a particular letter-string. Children can become intensely interested in words and their constituent parts if allowed to investigate in this way. Making links between words creates a framework by which the spellings of the words can be remembered.

The motor activity of writing also aids memory. It is considered that the fluid action of joining the letters is particularly effective. Copymaster 100 is provided to be filled out as in the example below:

| | sock |

ck	ck	ck	ck	ck	ck
sock					
sack					
sick					
lock					
back					
rock					
duck					

115

Suggested letter-strings and words which include them are listed below. The letter-strings and words may be written on to Copymaster 100 in the school's agreed handwriting style and then photocopied. Copymaster 101 contains pictures to illustrate the letter-strings and one of these should be stuck in the rectangle at the top of the sheet. It is not possible to illustrate all letter-strings with a picture. The children should trace over the letter-strings, and also write underneath on the lines provided. Similarly they should trace over and write the words containing the letter-string. Instructions for teaching the letter-strings are provided below. It is important that children read the words on these sheets. Learning to spell letter-strings divorced from the words that contain them misses the point of the exercise.

Some letter-strings can be embellished by amusing visual images. One obvious one is the word 'look'.

Children enjoy making up slogans, rhymes, riddles which use as many of the words from a string as they can, e.g. 'How now brown cow down there'. Pictures can be drawn to incorporate as many words from the string as possible, e.g. A sch*oo*l r*oo*m containing a b*oo*k with g*oo*d written on it, etc.

Some words prove difficult to remember by the methods already discussed and further devices may be required. For instance, some words lend themselves to letter-name chanting, a picture based on their shape or slogans or rhymes made up using each of the letters in order. These ploys need to be used sparingly. Too many can become confusing. If possible, children should be encouraged to make up their own. The process of doing so produces the thinking and often humour which makes the mnemonic unforgettable. Some examples are given below.

The most frequently used words as listed on page 107 may be grouped with other related words and taught as follows:

Words which may be correctly spelled by matching their sounds to appropriate letters

a	dad	him	not	then
an	did	if	on	this
at	dog	in	ran	up
bed	from	it	than	us
big	get	man	that	with
but	got	mum	them	yes
can	had			

When children write words 'as they sound' they will spell many words incorrectly, particularly the irregular words such as 'said' and 'was'. However, if children have been taught the sounds of the vowels (as shown in Part 1 Beginning to spell, pages 10–12) a number of common words will be correctly spelled such as 'not', 'them' and 'him'. While it becomes important for children to learn to amend the spellings of the most common irregular words, they must also be shown which words they *do* already spell correctly.

Words which may be correctly spelled by matching their sounds to appropriate letters, but where there is an irregularity or a different convention

> a) *Consonant 's' which sounds 'z'*
>   is, his
>   as, has
> b) *Vowels which have 'long' sound*
>   he, me, she, we, be
>   so, go, no, do, to
>   my, by, why, try
> c) *Consonants which 'double'*
>   back, sack, lock
>   will, hill, bell, full

a) Letter 's' sounding like a 'z' is very common particularly in plurals, e.g. 'design', 'flowers', 'lenses'. The letter 'z', on the other hand occurs infrequently. Children need to be aware of this.

b) In their early attempts at spelling, children sometimes add a 'y' to words such as 'he', and a 'w' to words such as 'go'. By grouping the 'e' words, children can see the similarities in spelling. If they have learned 'he' they can extend their knowledge to the other words in this group. Similarly, if they can spell 'to', which is a word most children learn very early, they can connect it to the others in the group even though they do not share a similar sound, i.e. they do not rhyme.

- **Copymaster 100**: letter-string 'e' (no picture).
Words: 'me', 'he', 'she', 'we', 'be'.
- **Copymaster 100**: letter-string 'o' (no picture).
Words: 'so', 'no', 'go', 'to', 'do'.
- **Copymaster 100**: letter-string 'y' (no picture).
Words: 'my', 'by', 'try', 'cry', 'why'.

c) Double consonants need to be learned as a convention.

- **Copymaster 100**: letter-string 'ck' (picture: sock).
Words: 'sock', 'sack', 'sick', 'back', 'rock', 'lock', 'duck', 'clock'.
- **Copymaster 100**: letter-string 'll' (picture: bell).
Words: 'bell', 'hill', 'doll', 'well', 'will', 'till', 'fill'.

Words which do not share a letter-string with any other frequently used words

have	made	make	because
saw	went	like	people
are	next	time	little
more	said	again	

went Young children find difficulty hearing the 'n' in 'went' and they often need it in their writing before they can hear the 'n', so it has to be learned as a visual form.

have No English words end in 'v'; 'live' is another example.

because Children feel very proud when they can spell their first long word. They like making up mnemonics. One boy made '**B**etty **e**ats **c**akes **a**nd **U**ncle **S**am's **e**ggs'. Another good example is '**b**ig **e**lephants **c**an **a**lways **u**nderstand **s**mall **e**lephants'.

116

Made, make, time, like This group of common four-lettered words all end in a modifying 'e'. It may be appropriate to point this out, 'changing the sound to its name'. However, children should practise writing each word. A poem about 'things I like' would give contextual practice.

people - 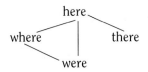 - a dog is a man's (people's) best friend. Chanting P-E-O-P-L-E (letter names) is a good idea.

more, are, saw, next These words need to be learned individually.

little This can make one long flowing movement under the hand if the 't's and 'i' are not crossed until the end. Again, saying the letter names as it is written is a good idea.

said This is a common word in which the pronunciation is different from the majority of words containing this vowel-string. Later on children may look into the connection between lay/laid, pay/paid and say/said, but initially this word needs to be learned as a visual form.

again In some accents the pronunciation of the 'ai' in 'again' is the same as the 'ai' in 'said' (agen, sed). Regardless of accent, the spelling pattern is the same, and chanting 'He *sai*d it *agai*n and *agai*n and *agai*n' can be useful in establishing a link between the two words.

Words which share a common letter-string

a) The following words share letter-strings which also sound the same. Some of these have been considered in Part 1 Beginning to spell. Although it is useful to know the possible spelling of certain sounds it is necessary to learn the particular spelling of each word, e.g. 'see' and 'sea' have different meanings. The letter-string 'ee' is included here because some of the most frequent words contain it, but in fact there are more 'ee' sounding words in the language which are spelled 'ea'. Teaching each letter-string should include class/group discussion, investigation and motor practice using Copymaster 100.

- **Copymaster 100**: letter-string 'ee' (picture: tree). Words: 'see', 'tree', 'been', 'seen', 'three', 'bee', 'queen'.
- **Copymaster 100**: letter-string 'ay' (picture: paying in a shop). Words: 'may', 'day', 'way', 'say', 'play', 'away', 'today'.
- **Copymaster 100**: letter-string 'ar' (picture: star). Words: 'party', 'part', 'far', 'hard', 'bar', 'barn', 'star'.
- **Copymaster 100**: letter-string 'all' (picture: ball). Words: 'all', 'call', 'ball', 'fall', 'tall', 'wall', 'small'.
- **Copymaster 100**: letter-string 'or' (picture: fork). Words: 'or', 'for', 'morning', 'form', 'born'.
- **Copymaster 100**: letter-string 'out' (no picture). words: 'out', 'about', 'shout'.
- **Copymaster 100**: letter-string 'ame' (no picture). words: 'name', 'came', 'same'.
- **Copymaster 100**: letter-string 'igh' (picture: lights). Words: 'night', 'light', 'might', 'right', 'bright', 'fight', 'high'.
- **Copymaster 100**: letter-string 'ow' (picture: cow) Words: 'how', 'now', 'down', 'brown', 'town', 'clown', 'crown'. Slogan: 'How now brown cow down there!'
- **Copymaster 100**: letter-string 'ir' (picture: rosette). Words: 'first', 'bird', 'girl', 'third', 'birthday'. Slogan: 'First the girl, then the boy; third the bird.'

b) In the following list a letter-string is not necessarily pronounced the same in all the words which share it. Some of the words can be grouped according to more than one letter-string. This may confuse some children, but may be interesting to others who are building up a wider picture of the language system.

- **Copymaster 100**: letter-string 'oo' (picture: look). Words: 'look', 'took', 'hook', 'book', 'good', 'school', 'door'. Slogan: 'He took a good look at the school'.
- **Copymaster 100**: letter-string 'er' (no picture). Words: 'after', 'water', 'over', 'her', 'very', 'ever', 'every', 'were'.

This letter-string is very common at the ends of words, and children enjoy spotting it in the middle of words and noticing the different pronunciation it receives (compare 'very' with 'every'). The spelling of 'every' can be helped by knowledge of the association. Children could be asked to underline the words containing the 'er' string in the following sentences:

We went there after dinner.
He took her over the water.
It is very hot in here in the summer.

- **Copymaster 100**: letter-string 'wa' (picture: wrist watch). Words: 'was', 'watch', 'want', 'wash', 'water'. Slogan: 'I want some water to wash.'

'wa' is the most common spelling of the sound 'wo'. It also occurs in 'swan', 'swamp', 'squabble', 'squad', 'squash' and 'squat' (which sound 'skw'). The only words in the dictionary to deviate are 'wobble', the slang words, 'wonky' and 'swot' and the proper nouns 'wok' and 'wombat'.

- **Copymaster 102**: letter-string 'the' (no picture). Words: 'the', 'then', 'there', 'these', 'them', 'they', 'their'. The recognition that all these words start with 'the' is a revelation to children who constantly spell 'they' as 'thay' and 'their' as 'thier'. There is of course a particular relationship in meaning between 'them', 'they' and 'their' which explains the common stem 'the'. Copymaster 102 is a worksheet with a 'the' wheel. The children should cut out the two parts and stick them on card. A paper fastener should be pushed through the black dot on the 'the' arm and attached to the wheel so that 'the' can be moved round the wheel to make the different words. Children can also practise writing these words.

- **Copymaster 100**: letter-string 'ere' (no picture). Words: 'there', 'were', 'here', 'where'.

'There' can also be viewed as an 'ere' word. Children enjoy playing around with these four words, drawing lines between common letters (three of them have 'here' in them, two have 'w', etc.).

```
          here
         /   |  \
  where      |   there
         \   |  /
          were
```

117

They can also make up conversations using and reusing these words, e.g.
'Where were they?'
'There? No, here.' etc ...
- **Copymaster 100**: letter-string 'ould' (no picture).
Words: 'could', 'would', 'should'.

- **Copymaster 100**: letter-string 'you', 'our' (no picture).
Words: 'you', 'your', 'our'.

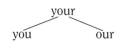

- **Copymaster 100**: letter-string 'an' (picture: man).
Words: 'an', 'and', 'man', 'many', 'any'.

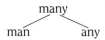

- **Copymaster 100**: letter-string 'on' (picture: one).
Words: 'on', 'one', 'once', 'only'.
Slogan: 'Once upon a time'.
The spelling of 'one' in no way conforms to children's earliest approach to spelling, yet it is a word which they see in books in the early stages and often need to write. Looking at the relationship in meaning between these words in terms of the common stem may be helpful. The danger is that they may put an 'e' in 'on(e)ly', particularly if 'lonely' is included.
- **Copymaster 100**: letter-string 'pu' (picture: push and pull).
Words: 'put', 'pull', 'push'.
The semantic relationship between these words may help children to spell them.
- **Copymaster 100**: letter-string 'as' (no picture).
Words: 'as', 'has', 'was', 'ask'.

Some children may find this connection helps them to remember 'was'. It is one of the earliest words children need to write and this connection may be more appropriate early on than the 'wa' letter string.
- **Copymaster 100**: letter-string 'ome' (no picture).
Words: 'some', 'home', 'come'.
You could include 'women' in this string but it would seem more logical to group: 'm*an*'   'm*en*'
                  'wom*an*'   'wom*en*'
- **Copymaster 100**: letter-string 'wh' (no picture).
Words: 'what', 'when', 'who', 'where', 'why', 'which'.
These are often referred to as the 'question words'.
Another way of presenting these words is in picture form:

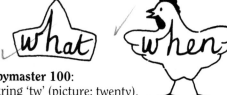

- **Copymaster 100**:
letter-string 'tw' (picture: twenty).
Words: 'two, 'twins', twenty'.
These words are connected in meaning by the stem 'tw'. It explains the spelling of 'two' where the 'w' is silent in pronunciation.
- **Copymaster 100**: letter-string 'use' (no picture).
Words: 'house', 'mouse', 'use', 'because', 'trousers', 'fuse', 'amuse', 'museum'.
This is an example of looking for a word within words. There are further examples of words within words on Copymasters 103–6.
- **Copymaster 103** Children should colour in the different words in the word 'there', circle the words in 'mother' and write words which they can see in 'something'.
- **Copymasters 104** and **105** Children should practise writing the words paying attention to the common letter-string. They can also colour the words 'one' and 'own'.
- **Copymaster 106** This copymaster gives children practice in distinguishing the letter-strings previously learned.

MORE LETTER-STRINGS

Many of the words and letter-strings introduced up to this point in relation to the most frequently used words also occur in longer words.
ay: 'today', 'yesterday', 'Monday', 'Tuesday' etc., 'display', 'dismay'
ome: 'become', 'women', 'aerodrome'
ere: 'sphere', 'atmosphere', 'interfere'
igh: 'lightning', 'mighty', 'delight', 'midnight', 'tonight', 'frightening', 'eight', 'eighth', 'eighteen', 'eighty', 'height', 'weight', 'freight', 'sigh', 'higher', 'straight'
tw: 'twice' and 'between'

Further letter-strings can be introduced:
ore: 'score', 'before', 'wore', 'adore'
ave: 'gave', 'save', 'brave', 'travel'
wor: 'word', 'worm', 'work', 'world', 'worse', 'worst', 'worth'

oes: 'does', 'goes', 'shoes', 'toes'
ough: 'though', 'although', 'through', 'thorough', 'enough', 'cough', 'tough', 'bough'
ought: 'ought', 'fought', 'nought', 'thought', 'brought', 'drought'
al: 'almost', 'although', 'altogether', 'also', 'always'
ound: 'found', 'round', 'around', 'ground', 'sound'
ear: 'ear', 'hear', 'hearing', 'heard', 'year', 'near', 'learn', 'earth'
be: 'because', 'before', 'begin', 'began', 'between', 'beside'

Other useful mnemonics are:
incident: the CID were called to the in*cid*ent
eye: (eye)
turn: U *tur*n in roads
knot: Ҡnot

118

FURTHER SPELLING PRACTICE

C107
–118

Spelling game I – Copymasters 107–9

Materials
Two copies of **Copymasters 107** and **108** and one copy of **Copymaster 109**.
48 red cards
24 blue cards
14 yellow cards
18 orange cards
16 green cards
All the cards should be the same size and no smaller that 8 by 6 cm.
Three trays
Pencil and paper for each child.
Plastic sentence stands (or made from folded card, stapled at each end, as shown below).

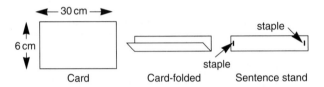

Preparation
Stick the words from Copymaster 107 on to the red cards and the words from Copymaster 109 on to the blue cards. Stick the words from Copymaster 108 as follows:

Yellow	Orange	Green
am	playing	out
is	looking	for
are	going	in
are	swimming	to
was	running	on
were	flying	at
were	sitting	by
	eating	with
	sleeping	

Spread the red cards out in one tray so that the words can be seen, the yellow in another and all the orange, green and blue cards in the third tray.

Activity
The children should check that they can all read the words.

Each child makes a sentence using the words in the trays as follows:

Red	*Yellow*	*Orange Green Blue*
1 or 2 cards	1 card only	any number of any colour

The sentences should be placed into the sentence stand so that other players cannot see them. Children decide order of turns. Child 1 reads his/her sentence, then rereads it word by word and the other players write it down.

The children check the spelling of the sentences they have written down against Child 1's version. Child 2 reads and then dictates sentence and so on.

Spelling game II for four children (using any collection of words, of groups of words): Copymasters 110 and 111

Materials
Selection of twelve words from **Copymasters 110** and **111** stuck on to playing cards. (Copymaster 110 contains three words from each of eight letter-strings; Copymaster 111 contains an unrelated selection of the most frequently used words.)
Box of counters
Pencil and paper for each player.

Procedure
Place cards face down in a pile in the centre of the table. Decide order of play. Player 1 takes a card from the pile and reads the word to the other players who then write it down. The card must not be shown to the other players. Player 1 checks the spelling of each player's word and gives a counter for a correct spelling. The card is then put face up next to the pile. Player 2 continues in the same way, etc. Used cards are piled face up next to the pile in play. The game is finished when all cards are used.

The strings game (for two to four children) using the following letter-strings: 'ould', 'ight', 'the', 'ome', 'ir', 'ow', 'all', 'ame', 'ay', 'oo', 'ee': Copymasters 112, 113, 114, 115 and 116.

Materials
Four baseboards (**Copymasters 112, 113, 114, 115**)
Nine counters for each player
Eleven word cards (**Copymaster 116**), each word stuck individually on playing cards.

Procedure
Each player has a baseboard and nine counters. Word cards are placed in a pile in the centre of the table. Player 1 turns over the top card in the pile. All players look at it and read it. Players should then look for a word on their baseboards which shares the same letter-string. If they find one they should put a counter on it. Player 2 turns over the next card, etc. The first player to cover nine words is the winner and when nine words are covered a pattern in the formation of the counters should be distinguishable.

Prefix and suffix wheels: Copymasters 117 and 118

Preparation
Stick **Copymasters 117** and **118** on to card. Cut out the wheels. Lay the middle-sized wheel on top of the largest wheel, and smallest wheel on top of the middle-sized wheel. Push a paper fastener through the centre.

Activity
Children should make as many words as they can using the affixes and stems.

Investigations

- Explore the number of words using the same stem, e.g.:

sign: 'signal', 'signify', 'signature', 'assign', 'design', 'resign' …

mne: 'mnemonic', 'amnesia' …

rupt: 'interrupt', 'interruption', 'rupture', 'corrupt' …

- Try to find a spelling convention with no or very few exceptions, e.g. 'i' before 'e' except after 'c'.

- Does the letter 'q' ever appear without 'u' in a word?
- Are there any conventions which might govern the use of the letter 'k'?
- Which vowels follow the hard 'g' and 'c' and the soft 'g' and 'c'?
- When are letters doubled?
- Make word webs, e.g.:

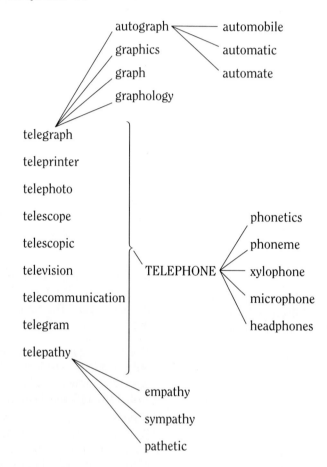

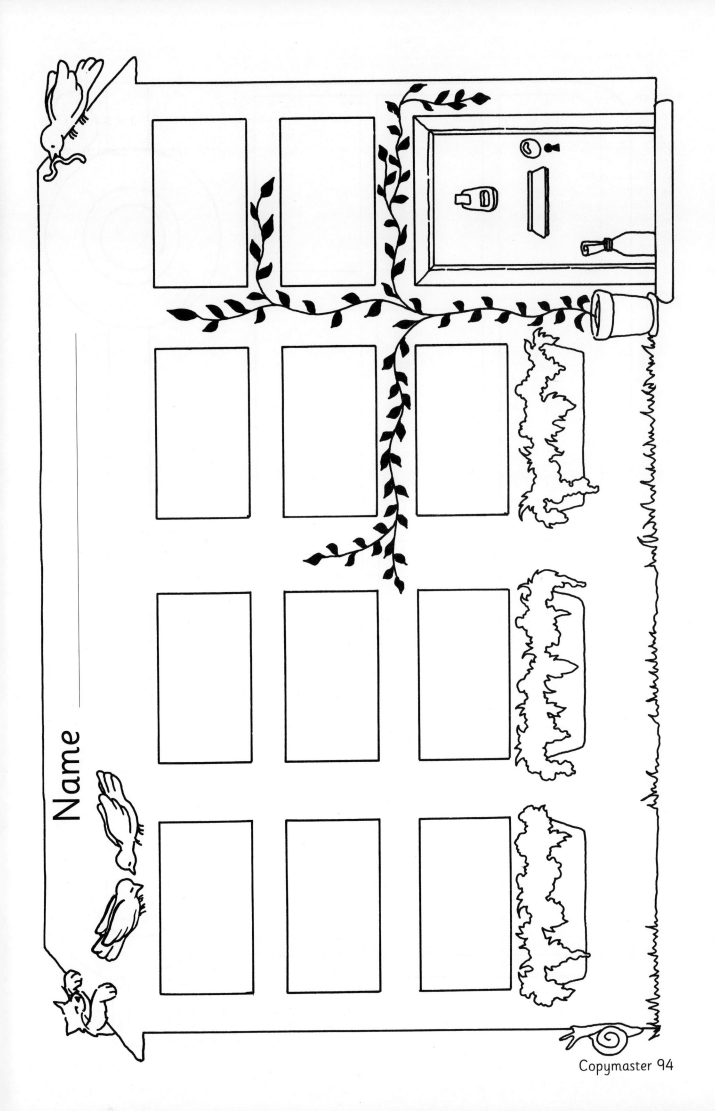

Name

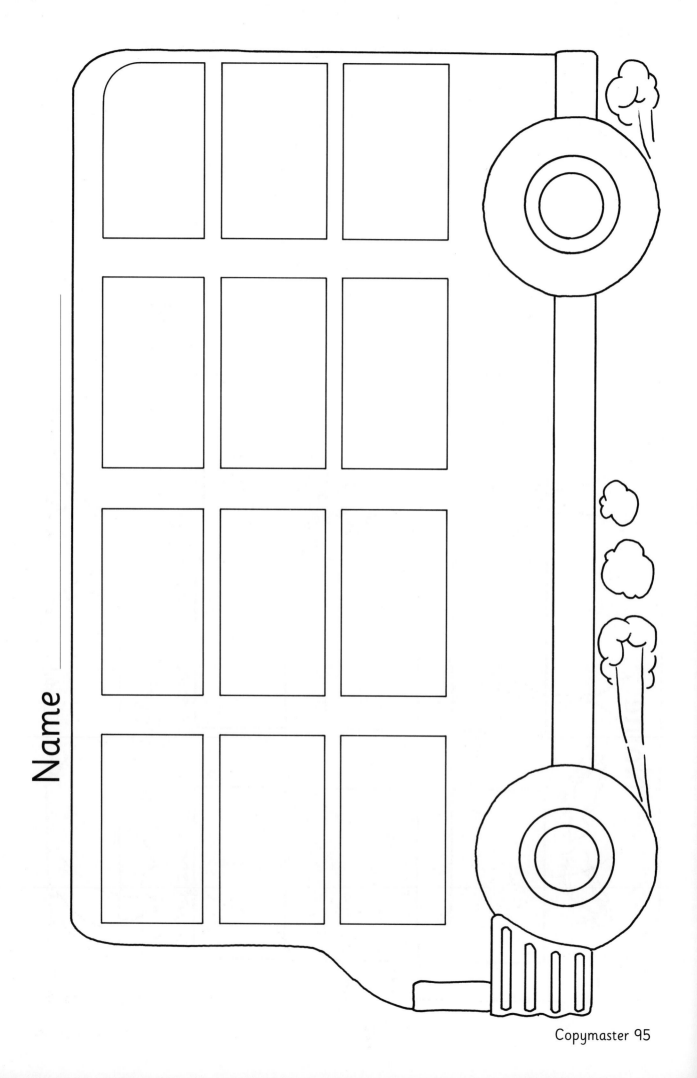

Name

Copymaster 95

Name _____

Name _____

SALE

Closing down _____ week

prices _____ £1

_____ for £1 | _____ for £1.50 | _____ for £2

_____ day of sale   prices right _____

£2 _____   _____ stock to go

home _____   good as _____

_____ home a bargain   _____ cheap

nothing _____ £5   _____ good to miss

Name _____

- _____ there lived a large brown rabbit in the side of a hill.
- He was very _____.
- He _____ no longer see very well.
- His children, grandchildren, great grand-children, nieces, nephews, great nieces and great nephews _____ to visit him.
- They told him stories of _____ adventures.
- _____ they had finished, he enthralled them with tales of his boyhood. He told them about the day he got shut in Mrs Scroggins' shed.
- He had crept in there _____ he was frightened. He was being chased by her dog.
- Mrs Scroggins had come to _____ him in for his supper.
- She had shut the door of the shed and gone _____ .
- He had not known what to _____ .

Name _____

The old rabbit had found himself shut in Mrs Scroggins' shed.

- 'Tell _____ what happened next', said all the younger rabbits.
- 'Well, I didn't _____ it much', said the old rabbit.
- 'There _____ lots of strange smells.
- 'I started to look for a means of escape. The _____ of the shed was rotten.
- 'I decided to _____ a hole in the rotten wood.
- 'I had just _____ gnawed a hole big enough to squeeze through when I heard a squeaking noise.
- 'So I _____ my eye to the hole.
- 'Right _____ the house I could see Mrs Scroggins' cat playing around with a mouse.
- 'I could see it would not _____ long before the cat ate the mouse.
- 'I did not _____ that to happen; nor did the mouse'.

Name

sock	watch	cow	lights
fork	look	tree	bell
one	man	twenty	star
pay	ball	first	push+pull

• the

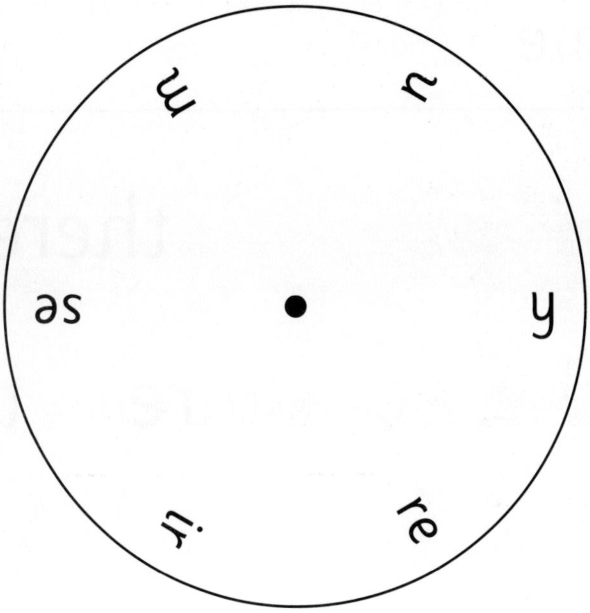

the

the   the   the   the   the   the   the

them   ___ ___ ___ ___ ___ ___

then   ___ ___ ___ ___ ___ ___

they   ___ ___ ___ ___ ___ ___

there   ___ ___ ___ ___ ___ ___

their   ___ ___ ___ ___ ___ ___

these   ___ ___ ___ ___ ___ ___

there

there   there   there   there

mother

1. mother   2. mother   3. mother

4. mother   5. mother

something

1. _____   2. _____   3. _____

4. _____   5. _____   6. _____

7. _____

Name _____

one

none money bone gone alone
stone lonely done phone

_____ none _____

_____ money _____

_____ bone _____

_____ gone _____

_____ alone _____

_____ stone _____

_____ lonely _____

_____ done _____

_____ phone _____

Name _____

own

down town clown crown drown

own flown grown blown

known sown thrown

down _____ own _____

town _____ flown _____

clown _____ blown _____

crown _____ grown _____

drown _____ known _____

sown _____

thrown _____

Name _____

one   own

cr_____   ph_____   m_____y

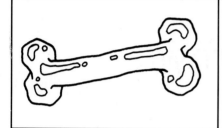

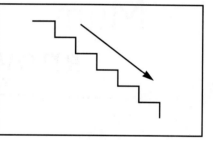

b_____   cl_____   d_____

	All the food has been eaten. There is n_____ left It has all g_____.
	He lived in a small t_____.
	The wind had bl_____ all the leaves off the trees.
	The little pig built his house of st_____.

I	you	she
he	we	they
Mum	Dad	It
The	A	boy
girl	dog	cat
and	the	My
my	moon	bird
The	and	the

107 107 107
107 107 107
107 107 107
107 107 107
107 107 107
107 107 107
107 107 107
107 107 107

am	is	are
108	108	108
are	was	were
108	108	108
were	playing	looking
108	108	108
going	swimming	sitting
108	108	108
flying	running	eating
108	108	108
sleeping	out	for
108	108	108
in	to	on
108	108	108
at	by	with
108	108	108

his	her	her
my	a	the
the	the	their
and	school	park
mum	dad	house
house	train	snow
seat	zoo	clouds
road	water	ball

109 (repeated on each card)

night	light	right
110	110	110
was	want	watch
110	110	110
could	would	should
110	110	110
may	day	way
110	110	110
put	pull	push
110	110	110
how	now	down
110	110	110
all	call	ball
110	110	110
what	when	who
110	110	110

have	saw	are
made	said	went
and	again	next
make	like	time
more	because	people
little	about	you
two	for	some
one	look	out

STRINGS GAME

my	good	has
call	saw	bird
because	should	people
down	he	some
did	light	yes
came	from	their

STRINGS GAME

same	people	right
because	come	saw
there	has	ball
my	girl	did
would	he	tree
from	good	yes

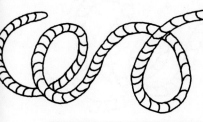 

STRINGS GAME

door	yes	from
same	girl	did
would	some	their
he	now	light
my	saw	day
has	because	people

STRINGS GAME

yes	from	did
door	bird	there
he	my	has
came	been	right
saw	because	people
come	way	should

home

name

the

all

see

night

how

look

could

first

may

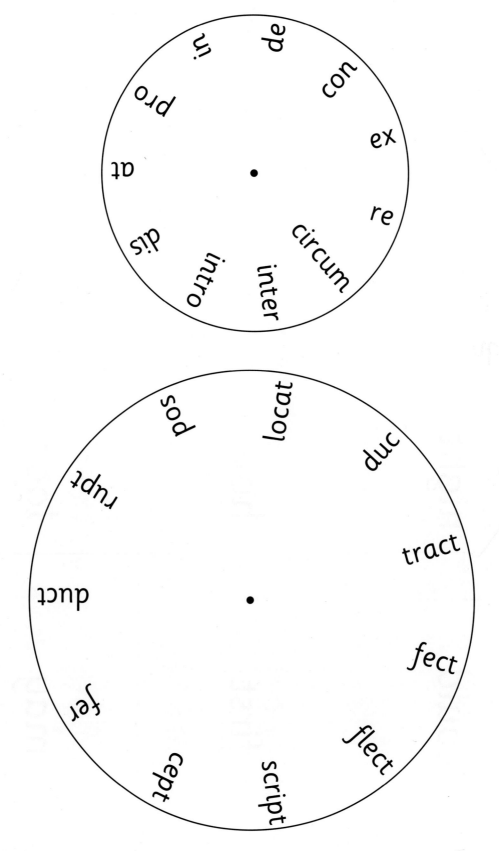

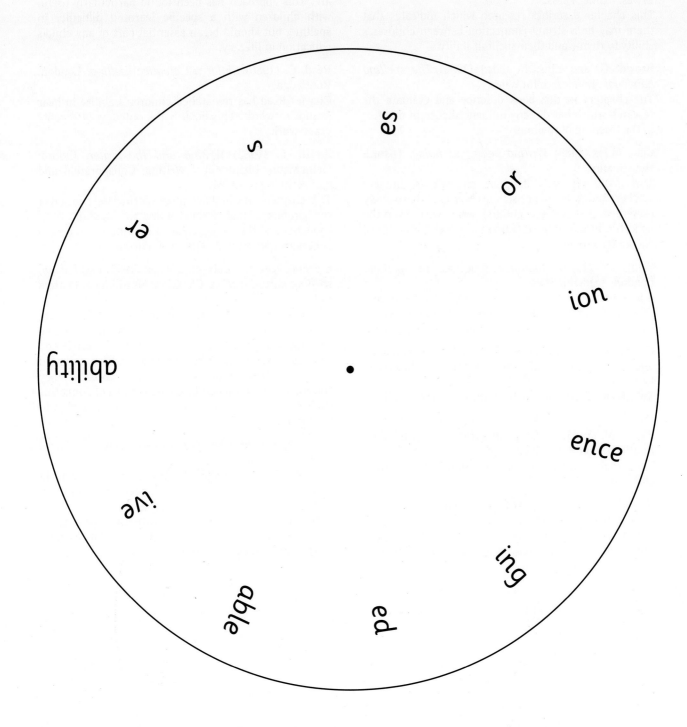

FURTHER READING

Bradley, L. (1990) Rhyming connections in learning to read and spell. In Pumfrey, P. and Elliott, C. (eds) *Children's difficulties in reading, writing and spelling.* Lewes: Falmer Press.
This chapter describes research which indicates that there may be a strong connection between children's ability to rhyme and their spelling ability.

Brown, G. and Ellis, N. (eds.) (1994) *The spelling handbook.* London: John Wiley.
The chapters in this book describe and evaluate the research which has directly influenced current practice in the teaching of spelling.

Clay, M.M. (1989) *Writing begins at home.* Oxford: Heinemann.
This book, primarily designed for parents, nursery teachers and carers of pre-school children, is beautifully presented. It shows how children write when given the opportunity and suggests ways in which children can be encouraged to do so.

Frith, U. (1980) *Cognitive processes in spelling.* London: Academic Press.
A presentation of the research picture at the beginning of the 80s, this book stimulated much further research, some of which is discussed in Brown and Ellis above.

Goswami, U. and Bryant, P. (1990) *Phonological skills and learning to read.* Hove, E. Sussex: Lawrence Erlbaum Ass.
This book discusses much of the recent research in spelling.

Peters, M. (1985) *Spelling: caught or taught.* London: Routledge and Kegan Paul.
This book emphasises the importance of teaching children to spell.

Ramsden, M. (1993) *Rescuing spelling.* Crediton: Southgate Publishers Ltd.
This book explains the importance of understanding the morphology and etymology of the language in learning to spell efficiently. Produced more with the KS2 child in mind, it lays the foundation for thinking about and exploring the reasons for words being spelled as they are. This approach has been found particularly useful with children with a specific learning difficulty in spelling, but should be an essential part of any child's education in literacy.

Read, C. (1986) *Children's creative spelling.* London: Routledge.
Charles Read has researched children's ability to hear sounds in words. This book is the outcome of twenty years' work.

Smith, F. (1982) *Writing and the writer.* Oxford: Heinemann. Chapter 3 – Writing: Collaboration and competition pp. 19–24.
This chapter is the best and most succinct description of the problems that writers have in juggling their thoughts and their knowledge of spelling to produce a coherent, well presented piece of writing.

Sterling, C.M. and Robson, C. (eds) (1992) *Psychology, spelling and education.* Clevedon: Multilingual Matters Ltd.
The proceedings of a conference in 1991 on spelling are contained in this book. The chapter entitled Invented spelling and learning to read by Huxford, Terrell and Bradley describes a research study which followed young children's progress in writing words as they sound. It showed that children are capable of doing this *earlier* than they can use the 'sounding out' method to read words.

Treiman, R. (1993) *Beginning to spell.* Oxford: Oxford University Press.
Rebecca Treiman analysed a sample of six-year-old children's writing in order to trace some common developmental patterns. Her findings from this and her other studies, in conjunction with those of Charles Read, constitute a solidly researched basis for teaching programmes in early spelling.